The Revolutionary Chat GPT Guide

How to Effectively Use AI Algorithm to Generate Human-Like Language; Better and Faster Writing, Increase Your Productivity, and Access Easier Income Strategies

Jenson Pena

Special Bonus!!
Want this bonus book for free?

Get **FREE** and unlimited access to it and all of my new books by joining the
Fan Base !

Table of Contents

Introduction

Consider this: you're at your desk, writing, and you're staring at a blank page with a blinking cursor. Deadlines are approaching, and you still can't get the words out of your head. What if, instead of struggling alone with your writer's block, you had access to a resource that not only comprehends language but can also produce it on the fly? The Artificial Intelligence (AI) language model ChatGPT is here to change all that.

Here in "The Revolutionary Chat GPT Guide," we'll go on an exciting adventure that combines the ingenuity of human language with the efficiency and accuracy of AI. This book is for anyone who wants to use artificial intelligence language models to improve their content generation, writing, and productivity. My mission is to equip you with the knowledge and skills necessary to use ChatGPT in a way that is consistent with ethical standards, allowing you to generate natural-sounding text, incorporate it into your writing process without any disruption, and discover new ways to make money.

I have designed this guidebook to accomplish three specific goals:

1. Improve the output and quality of writers and content creators by teaching them the ins and outs of ChatGPT and how to use it to its full potential.

2. Provide writers step-by-step instructions on how to include ChatGPT into their workflow and start using it to gain access to simpler income strategies.

3. Increase people's consciousness of the moral dilemmas posed by the widespread adoption of AI language models for writing, and provide guidelines for the ethical and responsible use of ChatGPT.

By the time you've finished reading this book, you'll have a deeper understanding of ChatGPT and how it may improve your writing. In addition to comprehending the constraints of the technology, you will get concrete skills for producing interesting, natural language. With this newfound information at your disposal, you will be able to maximize ChatGPT's potential and take your writing to new heights.

It's not only about becoming a better writer; there are simpler ways to make money, too. As you get more proficient using ChatGPT, you will find novel ways to make money, such as freelance writing and producing commercial content. This book will show you how to use AI language models to break into profitable markets and survive in the highly competitive content creation industry.

As the saying goes, "With great power comes great responsibility," it's important to think about the moral implications of employing AI language models in your work as you delve into ChatGPT's features. This book explores the moral implications of utilizing ChatGPT and provides guidance for doing so in a responsible manner. In order to traverse the murky waters of AI-driven content creation in a responsible manner, it helps to be aware of the potential repercussions and risks involved.

You will come to value the complementary nature of human ingenuity and machine learning as you work through this book. You'll get an understanding of ChatGPT's value as a resource for writers and learn to incorporate it into your workflow while adhering to the community's standards of conduct. Let's take the first step together on this thrilling journey to discover the full potential of AI language models.

Chapter 1

Getting Started with ChatGPT

In this chapter, I will give a thorough introduction to ChatGPT, detailing its main components and explaining how they work. We'll go back in time to see what came before ChatGPT in the family tree of artificial intelligence language models. In addition, I'll explain the many ChatGPT model types so that you can learn more about this groundbreaking technology and all the ways it can improve your writing and other forms of content production.

The History of AI-Language Models

Before digging into the history of ChatGPT, it is critical to comprehend the evolution of language models. When computers first appeared on the scene, they couldn't process human speech. Only instructions expressed in a programming language with precise syntax and grammar were able to be executed by a computer program.

Researchers started looking into techniques to make computers understand human languages with the introduction of Natural Language Processing (NLP). Among the first effective attempts at this were language models that could estimate the possibility of a sentence based on past text.

In the beginning, grammatical rules were employed by language models as a basis for interpretation. These models, however, had trouble processing more intricate and subtle forms of speech. The advent of neural networks allowed scientists to create more complex and precise models.

A Brief History of ChatGPT

OpenAI, a research organization established in 2015, is the genesis of ChatGPT. The group's mission is to advance AI for the greater good and create solutions that improve people's lives.

OpenAI revealed in 2018 that they had created a new language model dubbed GPT-1. The ability of GPT-1, a groundbreaking NLP system, to produce text that made sense in context was a major advance.

OpenAI started developing GPT-2, which is much more capable than GPT-1, after the success of GPT-1. However, because of ethical issues, OpenAI declared in 2019 that it would not release GPT-2. The group, however, decided to develop a scaled-down version of the model that might be made available to the general public. This model served as the backbone of ChatGPT and was given the name GPT-2-117M.

The Evolution of ChatGPT

The process of creating ChatGPT was difficult, requiring a lot of training and fine-tuning. The OpenAI team had to tweak the model, redesign the architecture, and add more training data to get ChatGPT to a point where it could produce high-quality answers to a wide range of questions.

The 2019 release of ChatGPT featured 117 million parameters. It was made to provide answers to many types of queries, statements, and even poetry. Since then, by adding more parameters and adjusting the architecture, OpenAI has continued to improve ChatGPT's capabilities.

As of its 2020 release, GPT-3 boasted 175 billion parameters, making it one of the most robust and comprehensive language models ever created. GPT-3's enormous processing power enables it to absorb and encode an unprecedented variety of linguistic nuances, resulting in writing that is not only logically sound but also appropriately situated. Because of this, GPT-3 has been shown to be an extremely useful tool in many contexts, such as chatbots, content production, code completion, and many more.

There are a number of reasons that have contributed to the lightning-fast development of AI language models. Increases in computing power are the first and most obvious factor in this development. Graphics Processing Units (GPUs) and Tensor Processing Units (TPUs) are two examples of high-powered processors that have made the training of complex models possible. As a result, these models can now pick up more nuanced representations of language.

Second, there is now an abundance of training data for AI language models because of the proliferation of digital text data. AI language models like GPT-3 have been able to absorb massive volumes of information, enhancing their knowledge of language patterns and structures, thanks to the internet's ever-expanding library of textual material.

Finally, major advances in algorithms have helped to boost AI language models. The development of transformer architecture, for example, has transformed natural language processing by enabling models to effectively capture long-range dependencies as well as contextual information in a text. Moreover, methods like task-specific fine-tuning and unsupervised pre-training have made it possible for AI language models to learn from both big datasets of unlabeled data and smaller datasets of labeled data more successfully.

The introduction of ChatGPT is a watershed milestone in the history of AI language processing systems. It has made great strides in the realms of language creation and understanding by employing novel pre-training and fine-tuning methodologies, in addition to a large number of computer resources.

As a result, the gap between machine-generated text and human-like language has narrowed significantly, opening up a plethora of opportunities for leveraging AI language models across various industries. For example, writers of content can now use ChatGPT to create original material, compose articles, or even complete books.

Similarly, ChatGPT-enabled customer care chat bots can improve user experiences and productivity by responding to questions with more precise and pertinent information.

The Different Versions of ChatGPT

Let's go over each model of ChatGPT and look at its features, strengths, and weaknesses. By looking at how ChatGPT has developed over time, we may gain insight into the progress of these AI language models and make educated predictions about their future.

GPT: The Genesis of a New Era in NLP

The first version of GPT was released by OpenAI in 2018. This innovative model was a radical departure from conventional NLP methods since it used unsupervised pre-training to absorb information from large quantities of textual input. This would allow the model to be fine-tuned for specific tasks using small amounts of labeled data, making it particularly effective at question answering, machine translation, and summarization.

Features:

- Developed methods for unsupervised training and tuning.

- Improved results across several natural language processing tasks.

Limitations:

- Compared to its successors, it is smaller and has less processing power.

- While the generated language made sense as a whole, it lacked the contextual relevance of later revisions.

GPT-2: Refining the Transformer Architecture

OpenAI followed up on the success of GPT with the 2019 release of GPT-2. Improved text production skills were the outcome of this model's expanded parameter set and modified transformer architecture. As a result of these concerns, OpenAI delayed the full release of GPT-2, which sparked a wider discussion about the ethical implications of sophisticated AI language models.

Features:

- More variables for better language comprehension.

- Enhanced capacity to generate text.

Limitations:

- The release date was pushed back because of safety concerns.

- The ability to generate contextually relevant text is still lacking, despite improvements in newer versions.

GPT-3: Massive-Scale, Natural-Sounding Language Creation

OpenAI introduced GPT-3 in 2020, making it the most cutting-edge version of the GPT line. With its staggering 175 billion parameters, GPT-3 established a new standard for artificial intelligence language models, proving it could produce logical and contextually relevant prose like never before. Many uses, including chatbots, content production, code completion, and more, have taken use of its flexibility and power.

Features:

- In-depth linguistic analysis using over 175 billion parameters.

- Exceptional writing skills that provide meaningful and consistent content.

- Wide range of potential applications.

Limitations:

- Uses a lot of computing power during training and implementation.

- GPT-3 has some great features, yet it can also generate illogical or biased results.

- The potential for abuse continues to raise ethical issues.

ChatGPT-4: The Next Step in Language Modeling

As of this writing, GPT-3 is the most recent stable release of ChatGPT. But, it's important to keep in mind that AI language models will certainly undergo further development, leading to the emergence of new versions of ChatGPT. Undoubtedly, these new models will improve upon prior versions, taking language comprehension and generation to new heights.

Expected Functions and Constraints:

- Further growth in model complexity and computational capability.

- Improved sensitivity to the nuances of language usage and context.

- Possible advancements in resolving biases and ethical problems.

- Problems arising from rising energy use and computing expenses.

The ChatGPT Model Spectrum

In this section, I'll go over the many ChatGPT model variants, what sets them apart, and where you may put them to use.

OpenAI's ChatGPT Models

Starting with the original GPT model, OpenAI has created numerous iterations of ChatGPT, including GPT-2, GPT-3.5, and the forthcoming GPT-4. OpenAI also provides GPT-Neo, another open-source option with lower computational requirements. Each new release improves upon its predecessors in terms of both language comprehension and output quality.

Adjusting Pre-Trained Models

To meet unique requirements, customers can fine-tune pre-trained ChatGPT models on their own datasets. These flexible AI language models can be used for a wide range of purposes, from content generation to question answering to summarization and beyond.

Third-Party Providers

ChatGPT models are provided not only by OpenAI but also by third-party vendors such as Hugging Face and EleutherAI. These services simplify the use of sophisticated AI language models by providing a wide selection of pre-trained models and intuitive interfaces to developers and researchers.

ChatGPT Models Tailored to Each Industry

ChatGPT versions can be specialized for use in fields like law and medicine, among others. These specialized models, which have been trained on domain-specific data, are able to produce higher-quality, more relevant content for their particular domains.

Choosing the Best ChatGPT Version

Many parameters, such as processing capacity, data availability, and the desired level of language comprehension and generation, determine which ChatGPT model is optimal for a given task. While larger models such as GPT-3.5 and GPT-4 can give more advanced features, their increasing computing demands may make smaller versions such as GPT-Neo more accessible to users with low resources. When choosing a ChatGPT model for a project, users should thoroughly evaluate their needs and the available options.

ChatGPT in Action: A Comprehensive Look

ChatGPT is reshaping the fields of language processing and content production with its wide array of available platforms, tools, and applications. Let's have a look at the various entry points and applications for ChatGPT to demonstrate its extraordinary adaptability and creative possibilities.

Platforms and Tools for Accessing ChatGPT

Users of varying technical proficiency can access ChatGPT thanks to its availability on numerous platforms and technologies. The following are just a few of the most common ways to connect to ChatGPT:

OpenAI's API

ChatGPT may be easily integrated into existing software and services thanks to OpenAI's Application Programming Interface (API).

Hugging Face's Transformers Library

Hugging Face provides a Python package called Transformers that makes it easier to interact with ChatGPT and similar artificial intelligence language models.

Google's Colab Platform

Users can deploy their Python programs in Jupyter Notebooks on Google Colab, a cloud-based platform. It's a great tool for exploring and deploying ChatGPT models, thanks to its pre-installed libraries and GPU support.

Applications of ChatGPT

Because of its exceptional language understanding and generation skills, ChatGPT can be used for a wide variety of tasks, such as:

Content Creation

ChatGPT can create high-quality, human-like material across a wide range of themes and writing styles, making it ideal for everything from article generation to social media post creation.

Chatbots

ChatGPT's contextual understanding and ability to generate natural-sounding responses make it ideal for developing conversational interfaces for customer service, e-commerce, and even entertainment.

Translation

ChatGPT can be used for translation, facilitating the smooth and precise exchange of text between speakers of various languages.

Summarization

ChatGPT helps users save time and focus by providing them with succinct summaries of articles, reports, and documents so that they may rapidly comprehend the key elements.

Compatibility With Other AI Tools

In addition to its use in language processing, ChatGPT has the potential to be combined with other artificial intelligence technologies to develop even more advanced software. Here are a few instances of such combinations:

Speech Detection

ChatGPT can enable voice-activated applications and virtual assistants when paired with speech-to-text systems that can create responses to voiced questions.

Image Processing

Artificial intelligence models that can comprehend and generate descriptions for images can be developed by connecting ChatGPT with computer vision algorithms, opening the door to uses such as automatic captioning and visual storytelling.

Multimodal AI

Developers can create multimodal AI systems by merging ChatGPT with other AI technologies; these systems can interpret and process information from numerous sources, including text, graphics, and audio, to provide more thorough and context-aware solutions.

Fine-Tuning ChatGPT for Maximum Performance

ChatGPT requires users to have an account with OpenAI or another source that provides access to the models. The normal procedure for creating an account entails the following:

- **Register for an account:** Users can create an account on the provider's website by filling in the usual fields (name, email, password).

- **Get an API key or access token:** After creating an account, users must request an API key or access token to begin interacting with the ChatGPT models. You can usually find this token or key in the provider's API docs or on their website.

- **Install any essential software:** Users may need to download and install supplementary programs or libraries in order to make use of ChatGPT, depending on the service provider and the specifics of the application. Python packages, CLI programs, and browser add-ons are all examples.

Modifying the ChatGPT Models

Users can start customizing the models for their needs as soon as they create an account and have access to the models. The term "fine-tuning" refers to the process of enhancing a model's performance by modifying its hyperparameters or adding new training data. The following are some of the most crucial features of tuning ChatGPT models:

Adjusting hyperparameters: The batch size, learning rate, and the number of training epochs are just a few of the hyperparameters that may be tweaked in ChatGPT models to improve their overall performance.

Training data: Users can contribute to the models' training by providing new data, hence expanding the algorithms' access to relevant examples. Depending on the context, this may include certain forms of text, such as medical reports, legal documents, or social media posts.

Model architecture: The number of layers, size of the embedding layer, and kind of attention mechanism in ChatGPT models can all be tweaked by the user to better suit the work at hand and the available resources.

Gains From Adaptive Modeling With ChatGPT

The benefits of fine-tuning ChatGPT models include the following:

- **Improved output accuracy and relevance:** The accuracy and quality of the output from ChatGPT models can be improved through fine-tuning in order to better understand and generate text that is relevant to a certain task or domain.

- **Improved efficiency in completing targeted objectives:** Users can improve performance on certain activities by modifying ChatGPT models for those tasks rather than using a general model.

- **Savings in computational expenses:** Users can get better outcomes with fewer resources by fine-tuning to reduce the amount of computation needed to train the models.

Chapter 2

Benefits of Using ChatGPT

This chapter delves into the various advantages of using ChatGPT, illuminating how it can improve the quality of written output, reduce the amount of time spent writing, and completely revolutionize the process of content creation. It also delves into the potential benefits of ChatGPT across a variety of sectors, highlighting its growing importance in the modern digital sphere.

In order to captivate their target audiences, content creators need to master the written word, which is the cornerstone of all other forms of communication. ChatGPT uses its GPT-4 architecture to tap into the vast potential of AI to aid in the creation of convincing and coherent writing while preserving the authorial voice and ethos. This chapter delves into the inner workings of this revolutionary technology to show how ChatGPT helps content creators get better at what they do while reducing the time spent on obstacles like writer's block and editing.

ChatGPT's versatility extends far beyond the realm of content creation, finding use in a wide variety of fields. From finance to healthcare and to marketing and customer service, this adaptable language model has the potential to rethink workflows, improve communication, and optimize decision-making processes across a variety of industries. In this section, we'll examine the ways in which ChatGPT can improve a wide range of industries, demonstrating how it can radically alter the ways in which people live, learn, and produce.

The Ultimate Creative Writing Companion

Writers in the creative writing genre face special difficulties in their attempts to captivate readers with compelling stories, construct interesting protagonists and antagonists, and paint evocative scenes using just words. ChatGPT, as a cutting-edge language model, provides a wide range of original solutions to these issues, allowing authors to expand their horizons in terms of self-expression, storytelling, and the like. Here, we explore the numerous applications of ChatGPT for improving the creative writing process.

Idea Generation

In creative writing, an idea germinates and grows into a multilayered tale. A writer's imagination can flourish in ChatGPT, which can provide numerous tale ideas and character possibilities. Writers can get a variety of suggestions that can serve as the basis for their work just by inputting a description or theme, which can then serve to stimulate their creativity and fuel their creative process.

Story Development

Creating a captivating story calls for careful work on the storyline, pace, and structure. ChatGPT can help with this by suggesting developments in the storyline, arcs for the story, and the driving forces behind the characters. ChatGPT allows writers to try out different narrative structures to find the most interesting and cohesive ones by displaying a succession of possible scenarios and outcomes.

Characterization

Having interesting characters is essential to any piece of writing, and ChatGPT can help you flesh them out. The AI model helps authors create believable and interesting protagonists by supplying them with in-depth character descriptions, backstories, and quirks. ChatGPT can also be used to help write natural dialogue, which is essential for bringing your characters to life on the page.

Setting and Worldbuilding

Careful consideration of the setting and the particulars that characterize it is essential for successfully transporting readers into the world of a novel. ChatGPT may provide writers with vivid descriptions, recommendations for interesting settings, and specific details that deepen the mood of their stories. Because of this, authors may create resonant worlds that feel authentic to their readers.

Overcoming Writer's Block

Writer's block is a common problem that can be frustrating for creative authors and cause them to lose faith in their abilities. When a writer is experiencing writer's block, he or she can turn to ChatGPT for a potent antidote in the form of new ideas, views, and word choices. ChatGPT can rekindle a writer's love for writing and help them push over creative roadblocks by providing a plethora of inspiration.

Editing and Revision

Refining a creative piece can be a time-consuming process, but ChatGPT can help speed things up by flagging errors, suggesting sentence-level adjustments, and boosting the text's overall flow and coherence. Writers can then concentrate on the imaginative components of their writing while ChatGPT takes care of the linguistic and stylistic details.

Content Marketing Reinvented

The proliferation of digital media means that there are now countless ways for brands to reach their customers. Effective marketing strategies now almost always include the production of high-quality content for various online mediums, such as blogs, social media, email campaigns, and websites. With ChatGPT's sophisticated linguistic skills, organizations and marketers may save time and increase the effectiveness of their digital marketing campaigns by automating the creation of engaging content for many platforms. In this article, we explore how to use ChatGPT to generate engaging posts for your website, social media, and other online marketing mediums.

Topic Analysis and Concept Development

It is essential for content development to first identify interesting themes and ideas that will appeal to specific audiences. As a means of generating ideas, ChatGPT can be queried for current topics, hot ideas, and sought-after terms. Marketers only need to enter a general category or sector of the economy to receive a plethora of suggestions that will resonate with their target demographic.

Designing Blog Posts

Putting together blog entries that are both educational and interesting can take some time. By producing outlines, suggesting subheadings, and supplying pertinent data points or statistics, ChatGPT can make this process easier. The blog content will be educational and interesting since the AI model can generate coherent, compelling, and high-quality language in the required tone and style.

Social Media Content

Maintaining an online presence and encouraging audience interaction in the dynamic realm of social media requires the constant production of new, interesting content. Concise, attention-grabbing language for captions, posts, and updates that is tailored to the specific needs of each social media site can be generated using ChatGPT to simplify this process. To further boost user engagement and content discoverability, the AI model may also help craft attention-grabbing headlines, CTAs, and hashtags.

Newsletters and Email Marketing

Email marketing is still highly effective, and ChatGPT can help companies and marketers craft more engaging and relevant emails for their consumers and subscribers. The AI model can come up with intriguing subject lines that get people to open the email, write persuasive prose that gets the point across, and create catchy CTAs that get them to do the required action.

SEO Optimization and Site Content

If you want more people to find your website and visit it because of the quality of its design and content, you need to optimize both. ChatGPT provides assistance in SEO content creation by suggesting keywords, meta descriptions, and picture alt text. The AI model can also create web material that is both user-friendly and educational, enticing readers to stick around and learn more.

Content Editing and Revision

Making sure material is correct, consistent, and easy to read across all platforms is a crucial part of any content strategy. Businesses and marketers can benefit from ChatGPT's editing and revision features since it flags grammatical faults, offers suggestions for better sentence structure, and improves the readability of the content as a whole.

Unlocking Global Communication

Language proficiency is rapidly becoming a necessity in today's globalized society. Language translation is an essential link in the chain of communication that binds together communities, industries, and nations. ChatGPT, being a state-of-the-art language model, boasts impressive capabilities in this area, enabling its users to translate text accurately between many languages with no effort.

ChatGPT is an effective translation tool because of its extensive knowledge base and nuanced understanding of languages. The AI model can take in material written in one language and output it in another, with the grammar, syntax, and idiomatic idioms that make each language distinct preserved in the translation. This guarantees that the translated text remains true to the meaning and context of the original, in addition to being cohesive and understandable.

ChatGPT's flexibility in meeting individual requirements is a major benefit when used for linguistic translation. By adding additional information, users are able to acquire translations that are specifically suited to their needs, whether they are translating a document for everyday use, a business setting, or a more technical subject like law, medicine, or the sciences. ChatGPT's adaptability means it may serve a variety of purposes, making it a valuable tool for both individuals and corporations.

ChatGPT's real-time translation capabilities are appealing because of how quickly and accurately they translate text. Users can acquire translations in a matter of seconds, allowing them to efficiently converse with people of diverse language backgrounds, gain access to resources written in other languages, and interact with audiences around the world.

Transforming Customer Support

Providing first-rate customer service is crucial to gaining and retaining customers in today's cutthroat business climate. ChatGPT's sophisticated language understanding and generating skills have tremendous potential to change customer service operations by allowing businesses to respond quickly, accurately, and individually to consumer inquiries and support tickets.

ChatGPT's capacity to create responses to common client inquiries in real-time is one of the most significant ways it may be used in customer support. The AI model can be integrated into existing customer care systems to speed up responses to client inquiries and reduce the burden on support staff. Increased customer satisfaction is the result of ChatGPT's ability to process and understand the context of customer inquiries, allowing for the creation of appropriate and relevant solutions that address the issue at hand.

ChatGPT's ability to tailor its responses to each individual user paves the way for conversation that is both warm and understanding. To make the customer feel like they've been heard and understood, the AI model can adjust its responses based on the tone, context, and urgency of the question. By showing compassion, businesses can increase customer satisfaction, loyalty, and brand affinity.

ChatGPT can aid customer care employees in solving complicated issues, in addition to answering common inquiries, thanks to its extensive knowledge base. Because of this, representatives can get the data they need fast and precisely handle customers' issues.

Organizations can save money by using ChatGPT in their customer service operations since it streamlines procedures and decreases the need for big support personnel. With ChatGPT, businesses can better allocate their customer care resources, guaranteeing that consumers receive high-quality support while reducing operational expenses by automating responses to simple inquiries and supporting agents with more complicated tasks.

Harnessing ChatGPT for Task Automation

To thrive in today's fast-paced and competitive corporate environment, it is essential to maximize efficiency and streamline procedures. Automation plays a crucial role in helping organizations save time, cut expenses, and boost productivity, particularly when it comes to the automation of typical writing chores. ChatGPT, with its sophisticated language production capabilities, emerges as a potent solution for automating a wide range of writing jobs, including content creation and customer service, freeing up time and resources to be applied elsewhere in the organization.

Businesses can reap significant benefits from automating the content generation process, which is an integral part of contemporary marketing and communication strategies. ChatGPT can reduce the time and effort needed to write material for social media, blogs, email campaigns, and web copy by generating text that is well-structured, coherent, and engaging. Businesses can ensure that their brand's voice and objectives are consistently and appropriately represented across all channels of communication by providing ChatGPT with detailed instructions.

ChatGPT's natural language processing capabilities make it ideal for automating answers to frequently asked queries and issues in customer service. The AI model may be integrated into existing customer care systems to improve response times and accuracy while reducing stress on support staff. As a result, both customer satisfaction and the efficiency of customer care operations improve as support workers are freed up to tackle more complicated challenges.

ChatGPT's task automation capabilities are not limited to just content creation and customer service; the software can also be used to streamline the process of drafting reports, summarizing meetings, and analyzing data. ChatGPT helps firms save time and money by streamlining a variety of processes so that staff can devote more attention to jobs that need analysis, innovation, and planning.

Building a More Inclusive and Equitable Digital World

Accessibility for individuals with impairments is a critical component of establishing inclusive and fair experiences in today's increasingly digital environment. By allowing speech-to-text and text-to-speech conversion, ChatGPT can help more people gain access to information, interact with the material, and communicate effectively, thanks to its sophisticated language interpretation and generating capabilities.

Those who have trouble hearing need the ability to convert speech to text so they can read what they've heard. By considering subtleties of speech like intonation, pace, and regional accents, ChatGPT is able to transcribe spoken language into written text with exceptional accuracy. This removes barriers and makes sure that everyone can make use of the richness of information available online by allowing users to access content from audio-based media like webinars, podcasts, lectures, and more without relying on aural cues.

Text-to-speech conversion, on the other hand, is crucial for those who are blind or have trouble reading since it provides them with access to written content through aural methods. ChatGPT's sophisticated language generation capabilities allow it to accurately translate written text into conversational speech while preserving its structure, meaning, and tone. This guarantees that reading articles, books, and documents can be a pleasant and easy experience for users.

Because of its flexibility, ChatGPT can process and output content in a number of languages, making it accessible to users with a wide range of linguistic backgrounds and preferences. Because of this, it is a priceless tool for accommodating the requirements of people with disabilities who speak non-mainstream languages or dialects in a way that is both powerful and respectful.

Shaping the Future of Journalism

The ability to consistently produce high-quality, timely, and relevant information is essential for media outlets in today's competitive media landscape if they want to preserve their credibility and audience base. ChatGPT's sophisticated language understanding and generating skills have the ability to radically alter the state of journalism by helping reporters and news outlets increase output without sacrificing quality or accuracy.

News stories and articles can be generated using ChatGPT and fed raw data from sources, including press releases, interviews, and research papers. The AI model is able to process these sources, extract relevant information, and synthesize it into narratives that are compelling, logical, and informative. ChatGPT takes care of the preliminary drafting process, freeing up journalists to focus on in-depth research, investigative reporting, or feature writing.

You can use ChatGPT to create anything from news bulletins and summaries to opinion pieces and feature-length articles. By instructing the AI model in a certain way, journalists can get content that fits with their editorial goals and the interests of their readers, resulting in reliable, high-quality work across all mediums.

Fast reactions to breaking news are critical in today's instantaneous media environment. As ChatGPT can generate information quickly, news organizations may keep their audiences up to date by reporting on events as they happen. In turn, this serves to establish media outlets as trustworthy and timely information providers, winning over and keeping devoted audiences.

Furthermore, media outlets can increase their coverage and reach varied audiences because of ChatGPT's capacity to process and generate information in multiple languages, helping to foster greater inclusion and global understanding. Journalists can more successfully reach a wider audience and cover a wider range of topics by leveraging the AI model's linguistic capabilities and removing language barriers.

Streamlining the Coding Experience

Successful software development relies heavily on speed and precision. ChatGPT's powerful comprehension of natural languages and generation features have the potential to revolutionize the way developers write code by automating tedious tasks like code generation and auto-completion.

ChatGPT can produce code snippets from natural language descriptions, which is a huge benefit when utilizing it for coding. ChatGPT is an artificial intelligence model that can be fed plain English descriptions of desired functionality from developers. This not only simplifies the coding process but also frees up time for developers to work on more high-level concerns like software architecture and design.

ChatGPT's auto-completion is another excellent tool that can considerably improve developers' time spent working. ChatGPT can predict the developer's purpose while they type and then offer the next best keywords, variables, or functions. This not only helps save time by decreasing the number of keystrokes required, but it also aids in lowering the number of syntax errors and other typical blunders, resulting in more streamlined and effective code.

For developers dealing with a wide variety of technologies, ChatGPT's ability to comprehend and generate code in different languages is invaluable. Developers' productivity, flexibility, and ease in learning new languages and frameworks can all benefit from the AI model's linguistic ability.

As a result of its familiarity with the codebase and the expected features, ChatGPT is also able to offer guidance in tracking down and addressing faults in existing code. This has the potential to result in more stable and secure software, with fewer bugs and a better overall experience for end users.

Revolutionizing AI in Legal & Financial Writing

Law and finance are notoriously demanding professions, with experts frequently dealing with sophisticated, time-consuming document-generating responsibilities. ChatGPT's sophisticated language interpretation and generating skills have enormous potential to transform legal and financial writing by allowing attorneys and analysts to quickly and accurately produce high-quality documents, including contracts, reports, and proposals.

In the field of law, ChatGPT can be used to create legally binding documents like contracts and agreements in accordance with predefined parameters. Legal practitioners can produce well-structured, clear, and legally sound drafts that comply with the applicable rules and regulations by feeding the required information and intended outcomes to an AI model. This not only improves efficiency but also lessens the possibility of mistakes, freeing up lawyers' time for more high-level strategic considerations.

ChatGPT can be used by financial analysts to produce in-depth reports, ideas, and assessments that are true to the data at hand. The

AI model is able to provide material that is not only useful and accurate but also interesting and simple to grasp by digesting complex financial data and extracting crucial insights. Better decision-making and outcomes are possible as a result of financial professionals' enhanced ability to convey their findings and suggestions.

In fields like law and finance, where accuracy and formality are essential, ChatGPT's ability to keep a document's tone and style consistent is invaluable. By utilizing the AI model's language-generating skills, experts can make sure their documents are up to par with all the rules and regulations that matter.

Optimizing Data Analysis in Research

The ability to evaluate and generate meaningful text from massive datasets is vital in the ever-expanding realm of scientific research and data-driven fields for extracting significant insights and increasing knowledge. ChatGPT's superior language recognition and creation skills can help researchers and professionals extract relevant insights and cohesive narratives from enormous datasets.

When used in conjunction with large datasets, ChatGPT can help researchers spot trends, correlations, and other patterns that might otherwise go unnoticed. The AI model can quickly and accurately handle large amounts of data to provide researchers with a complete grasp of the phenomena, allowing them to focus on deeper investigation and hypothesis testing.

ChatGPT can be used for more than just analyzing data; it can also be used to write study summaries, abstracts, and even full-length publications. By feeding the data and insights into the AI model, scientists can generate narratives that are both informative and interesting, perfect for sharing their findings with the scientific community and expanding the body of knowledge. In addition to being a time-saver, this facilitates the rapid and extensive dissemination of research results.

In addition, ChatGPT's multilingual content processing and generation capabilities improve cross-cultural communication and cooperation in the scientific community by removing language obstacles to information exchange. Researchers can efficiently transcend language barriers and interact with a wide spectrum of knowledge by utilizing the AI model's linguistic capabilities.

Empowering AI Content Creation

The modern marketing landscape is highly competitive, so firms need to develop high-quality, persuasive content to attract and retain customers. ChatGPT's sophisticated natural language interpretation and generating skills have enormous potential to change the production of marketing content, allowing businesses to rapidly and accurately produce engaging advertising, product descriptions, and other marketing materials.

ChatGPT's ability to generate personalized and interesting content that connects with certain target audiences is a major selling point for the platform. By feeding the AI model data on the demographics of the target audience and the objectives of the marketing campaign, businesses may generate content that is targeted to those customers' specific wants, requirements, and pain points.

Also, ChatGPT's language generation features can be used to make headlines, taglines, and calls to action that grabs the attention of potential customers and gets them involved with the brand. Marketers may use the AI model's knowledge of language and persuasion strategies to craft engaging content that attracts the attention of target audiences, gets shared widely, and ultimately leads to the success metrics they've set.

ChatGPT's ability to provide content in more than one language helps businesses reach and interact with customers all around the world. Marketers may expand their brand's reach and market penetration by taking advantage of the AI model's multilingual capabilities to localize content and tailor messaging to the cultural and linguistic preferences of their target audience.

Breaking Down Barriers in Education

It is more important than ever to have readily available, high-quality, and interesting educational materials in today's constantly-evolving educational landscape. ChatGPT's excellent natural language interpretation and generating skills can help educators and content creators develop training manuals, textbooks, and course materials, faster and more accurately, increasing global access to education.

ChatGPT's capacity to produce content that follows prescribed criteria and pedagogical tenets is a major selling point for its use in the classroom. By feeding the AI model data about the learning goals, audience demographics, and topic at hand, teachers may generate interesting and relevant materials that help students grasp difficult topics in a way that works for them.

The ability to generate content in many languages is another strength of ChatGPT, allowing teachers to develop lessons that can be understood by students of all linguistic backgrounds. Creators may effectively reach students from a variety of cultural and linguistic backgrounds by taking advantage of the AI model's multilingual ability to localize materials and alter messaging to resonate with students from those backgrounds.

A further benefit of adopting ChatGPT for education is its compatibility with other technologies, such as interactive digital tools and e-learning platforms, to produce immersive and individualized learning experiences. By using the AI model's ability to generate language, teachers can create content that changes based on each student's needs and progress. This way, each student gets the right help and guidance to reach their learning goals.

Chapter 3

Challenges of Using ChatGPT

It is essential to recognize and handle the possible issues connected with the use of ChatGPT as its acceptance continues to expand across a wide range of industries and applications. This chapter explores the major drawbacks and restrictions of ChatGPT, explaining in depth the problems with precision, bias, and ethics that it faces. By being aware of these challenges, users will be better equipped to make educated decisions about how to deploy and oversee ChatGPT, leading to a more ethical and productive usage of the platform.

Accuracy

While ChatGPT's accuracy is remarkable in many situations, it may present some difficulties for users, especially when working with more complicated or technical text. ChatGPT is an artificial intelligence language model that, thanks to its extensive training data, can generate natural-sounding writing. However, the model's knowledge is intrinsically limited by the quality and extent of its training data. Therefore this data-driven strategy does not ensure the provision of accurate or reliable information in all scenarios.

When it comes to accuracy, ChatGPT has been criticized for producing writing that sounds natural and flows well but really contains mistakes or misinterpretations. This can be especially troublesome in highly specialized or technical fields, where familiarity with certain jargon and concepts is essential for conveying meaning. Some of the efficiency improvements promised by the technology may be offset by the time and effort users must expend to examine and modify the information generated by AI.

Another issue with precision is that ChatGPT often produces irrelevant or inconsistent content. Since the model mostly depends on patterns in the training data, it could find it difficult to sustain a logical story or argument throughout the course of a lengthier piece of text, leading to content that seems disconnected or contradictory. Users that rely on reliable data for crucial purposes like decision-making, research, and the like may find this problem particularly frustrating.

Moreover, ChatGPT's inability to grasp specialized terminology, industry-specific concepts, and cutting-edge trends or technology may contribute to the inaccuracy of the information it generates. Even when the AI model has been trained on a wide variety of texts, it may still lack sufficient or out-of-date information in certain areas, resulting in the production of content that does not accurately reflect the level of knowledge or practice in a certain sector.

Bias

The possibility for biases in both language and content to be perpetuated is one of the key issues that come along with adopting ChatGPT. ChatGPT, like an AI language model, is trained on a large body of data that necessarily contains biased or prejudiced examples. As a result, there is a risk that the AI model would unwittingly reproduce and magnify these prejudices, which could have negative consequences for both the intended and unintended audiences.

Biases in ChatGPT can manifest in a variety of forms, from those based on race and gender to those based on culture and politics. The AI model could produce material that promotes discriminatory ideas or views, for example, by reinforcing gender stereotypes, displaying racial prejudice, or the like. Such prejudices can distort the generated material, making it less credible and more likely to upset the intended audience.

ChatGPT's potential for its AI model to produce politically biased or controversial content is another bias-related issue. Due to the diversity of perspectives represented in the training data, it is possible that the model will provide politically divisive results in spite of its intended purpose. This is especially difficult in formal or delicate settings where objectivity and objectivity are of the utmost importance.

In addition, ChatGPT's inherent cultural biases may inspire writing that ignores or trivializes the richness and subtlety of various cultural settings. The AI model could unintentionally promote cultural insensitivity by reinforcing preconceived notions through its reproduction of stereotypes or misrepresentation of cultural behaviors.

To overcome these challenges, it is essential for ChatGPT's creators and users to be conscious of the possibility of biases in the created content and to take steps to limit their impact. Engineers may refine the AI model's training data and techniques to reduce bias, while users can use diligent content inspection and editing to discover and rectify biased language and opinions. ChatGPT users can more ethically and responsibly utilize this potent AI-driven solution by tackling the issue of bias head-on, making for material that is not only interesting and instructive but also diverse and fair.

Quality

While ChatGPT has received a lot of praise for its capacity to generate natural-sounding English, it may provide its users with a substantial issue in the form of inconsistent quality in its AI-generated output. The generated text may not always reach the high standards needed for professional writing or journalism, even though the AI model can produce logical and presumably well-structured information. This difficulty shows how artificial intelligence-driven content generation solutions fall short in situations where quality, believability, and nuance are crucial.

The tendency of ChatGPT to produce shallow content devoid of critical examination is one source of the platform's quality problems. While the AI model was built to replicate human language, it may lack the subtle knowledge and perspectives seen in well-written academic papers or news articles. So, the AI-generated material may come out as generic or bland, unable to captivate its audience or provide anything of substance.

The possibility that ChatGPT will produce information that is repetitive, too verbose, or lacking in clarity is another quality-related worry. Since the AI model's first priority is to generate writing that sounds natural and makes sense, it may occasionally generate information that puts fluency ahead of brevity or clarity. Professional writing and journalism are two genres where this problem often rears its ugly head since clarity, brevity, and concentration are crucial to presenting information effectively and keeping readers' attention.

It's also possible that ChatGPT's generated content will suffer from an inconsistent tone, style, or voice, which will lower the quality and make it harder to read. Establishing credibility, establishing a connection with the audience, and effectively communicating the message all depend on the writer or journalist having a consistent voice.

ChatGPT users will need to adopt a critical stance toward user-generated content and be willing to devote time and energy to evaluating, revising, and improving the output in order to overcome these quality issues. Users can improve the quality of the AI-generated text and ensure that it meets the requirements of professional writing or journalism by injecting human skill and judgment into the content generation process. The key to fully realizing ChatGPT's potential rests in adopting a collaborative strategy that blends the capabilities of both AI-driven solutions and human expertise, taking advantage of both its superior linguistic capabilities and its inherent limits.

Ethics

ChatGPT's use as a content creation tool brings up a number of moral questions for its users, specifically concerning issues of accuracy, accountability, and transparency. The increasing indistinguishability of AI-generated content from human-written text raises ethical concerns, underscoring the need for responsible and transparent approaches while employing ChatGPT in a variety of applications.

The question of authenticity raises serious moral questions about the employment of ChatGPT. The ability of the AI model to generate content that is both novel and human-sounding can make it difficult to tell the difference between real human expression and computer-generated language. Because of this, there is cause for fear that readers may lose faith in the veracity of written content since they are unable to verify its authenticity. To solve this problem, people using AI need to be extra careful that the content they create and share does not violate anyone's rights to their intellectual property or misrepresent who wrote it.

Responsibility is another important aspect of using ChatGPT ethically. It can be difficult to ascertain who is to blame when an AI model produces information that is biased, deceptive, or damaged without any human participation. Users can get around this difficulty by instituting stringent procedures for reviewing and modifying content before it is shared publicly. Furthermore, in order to ensure that accountability is upheld throughout the content creation process, developers and users must collaborate to define standards and best practices for the ethical deployment of ChatGPT.

Addressing the ethical concerns surrounding ChatGPT relies heavily on transparency since informing readers and stakeholders about the usage of AI-generated content is crucial to building trust and protecting the veracity of the information being disseminated. By being forthright about their usage of ChatGPT, users can allay ethical concerns and encourage honest discussion about the promise and limitations of AI-generated material.

Creativity

Despite ChatGPT's impressive performance in creating natural-sounding language, it is important to remember that it cannot replace human ingenuity. The main problem with relying on ChatGPT for content creation is that it lacks flexibility and creativity. The AI model may be capable of advanced language processing, but it may lack the creative expression and cleverness that is present in human writing.

ChatGPT's inherent artificial intelligence (AI) model constraints severely limit its inventiveness. It is intrinsically dependent on pre-existing content because it learns from a massive database of human-generated text. As a result, the AI model can have trouble coming up with novel concepts or stories that break away from the familiar structures and patterns it encountered during training. The content it generates may appear consistent and relevant, but it may lack the human ingenuity that distinguishes truly original works.

The difficulty of innovation in ChatGPT also stems from the fact that it cannot completely understand and interact with deep emotional, experiential, and cultural aspects. ChatGPT, being a machine learning model, isn't equipped to create material with the same level of emotional resonance and cultural sensitivity as humans are. Because of this restriction, writers may produce work that lacks depth and fails to resonate with their audience.

In addition, as ChatGPT uses pre-existing patterns and structures, it may produce content that is overly simplistic or predictable. The AI model may be very good at mimicking human language, but it may not have the same capacity as human writers to break with convention or test the limits of creative expression.

In light of these obstacles, it is critical for users to be aware of the restrictions placed on them by ChatGPT. Users should not see ChatGPT as a replacement for human creativity but rather as a resource to be leveraged in addition to human knowledge and ingenuity. Users can create material that is interesting, unique, and fresh by working together to make use of the AI model's linguistic capabilities and the special creative potential of human writers.

Context

A big problem with using ChatGPT to make content is that it needs to be able to understand the context of a writing task and adapt to it, as well as make content that is relevant and right for the audience. But, the AI model's language skills aren't perfect; it may occasionally produce information that is inconsistent, off-target, or inappropriate since it doesn't understand the subtleties of context or respond to the specific demands of a target audience.

The difficulty ChatGPT has in understanding the context of more nuanced and sophisticated writing tasks is one source of that difficulty. This is because, as a machine learning model, it makes assumptions about the nature of the writing task based on the patterns and structures it observes in its training data. As a result of this restriction, content may be generated that is not optimal for the intended audience or situation.

ChatGPT also struggles with context because it cannot always understand the goal of a writing activity, which might affect the quality of the output. For instance, the AI model may have trouble telling the difference between an argument and an analysis, or it may misjudge the appropriate level of formality or informality for a given audience.

Content that isn't well-suited to its goal or doesn't resonate with its intended audience is the result.

Furthermore, the acceptability and efficacy of the generated content may be affected by ChatGPT's lack of expertise in handling information that is culture-specific or context-dependent. Because the AI model can only learn what it sees in its training data, it may produce material that doesn't entirely fit its context or appeal to its target audience because it doesn't comprehend cultural nuances, regional variances, or audience preferences.

Contextual difficulties can be overcome if users examine ChatGPT-generated content critically and are willing to put in the time and effort to modify the output so that it better fits the needs of the intended audience and the given context. The language capabilities of the AI model can be leveraged in tandem with human knowledge and judgment to produce results that are relevant, appropriate, and suited to the specific needs of the intended audience.

Control

Controlling the results produced by the AI language model is a significant obstacle when employing ChatGPT for content development. ChatGPT's ability to generate natural-sounding language is promising, but it has the potential downside of producing content that doesn't match the user's goals or preferences. This uncertainty can be frustrating for users who are attempting to use the

AI model to produce work that is both high quality and suitable for its intended context.

This difficulty arises mostly because AI language models learn from enormous amounts of human-generated material. So, the output of ChatGPT is impacted by its training data, and it might not match the user's preferences. This can lead to the production of content that is irrelevant, contradictory, or otherwise unfit for consumption.

ChatGPT's shallow familiarity with its own output further complicates efforts to exert authority over it. The AI model may be able to effectively imitate human language, but it may lack the comprehension and intent of a human writer. This might cause the production of a text that, at first glance, seems cohesive but, upon closer inspection, turns out to be inconsistent with the user's original intent.

Since the AI model behind ChatGPT has the potential to produce biased, inflammatory, or otherwise improper content, regulating its output can be difficult. Artificial intelligence models run the risk of perpetuating detrimental biases and language patterns from their training data, which might lead to inappropriate or irrelevant results for the user.

Users must be watchful and proactive in analyzing and modifying the output supplied by ChatGPT to address the control-related issues that arise. Users may make sure the final product is consistent, suitable, and aligned with their intended message by carefully reviewing the AI-generated content and making any necessary edits. Also, developers need to hone and enhance the AI model's capacities so that it can better comprehend and react to human input, giving users finer-grained command over the content-generating process.

Complexity

Despite ChatGPT's impressive track record in language production, it's important to keep in mind that it's a sophisticated technology with its own set of limitations that could prevent it from being used by some people. To deploy and use ChatGPT well, you need some technical skills and knowledge. This may be a problem for some writers or businesses that want to use the power of AI language models to create content.

Challenging aspects of ChatGPT include learning to read the blueprints of AI language models and navigating their training data and capabilities. If they want to make the most of the AI model while also understanding its limitations, users need a firm grasp of these facets. This could mean devoting effort and resources to studying artificial intelligence (AI) technologies, gaining relevant expertise, and keeping up with advances in the field.

In addition, optimizing the AI model for a particular writing activity or setting is a common practice when utilizing ChatGPT. Understanding the characteristics and capabilities of an AI model is essential for this procedure, which can be time-consuming and difficult. Fine-tuning may involve changing the model's training data, architecture, or configurations to get the desired result, which requires technical expertise.

ChatGPT's complexity, and that of other AI language models, may also provide logistical and financial hurdles. The time and effort required for deploying and maintaining such models may exclude their usage by those without sufficient financial or technological means. This can lead to inequalities in the availability of AI-powered content production platforms, such as ChatGPT, making it difficult for smaller enterprises or individual writers to fully utilize its capabilities.

To solve ChatGPT's complexity issues, education and capacity-building must be prioritized to teach more users how to use AI language models. The creation of ChatGPT interfaces that are both more intuitive and less demanding of technical knowledge can further break down entry barriers and make this potent tool more accessible to a larger variety of users.

Legal Considerations

The legal ramifications of using AI-powered language models like ChatGPT are becoming increasingly important as they become more integrated into the content creation process. ChatGPT users who are trying to act properly and ethically when employing the AI model may encounter difficulties connected to plagiarism, intellectual property, and copyright when generating material.

The topic of who owns the ideas generated while utilizing ChatGPT raises important legal concerns. The increasing sophistication and human-like quality of AI-generated material raises the question of who owns the intellectual property rights to this content. There is still no clear answer to the question of who, if anyone, should be credited as the producer of work generated by an AI system; this has serious ramifications for both individual creators and businesses.

Copyright infringement is another legal concern because ChatGPT uses large amounts of user-generated content to learn language structures and patterns. Copyright rules may be broken if the AI model accidentally uses terms or sentences from its training data in the created output. Users need to be careful to evaluate and alter AI-generated content for any infringements on copyrighted works.

When creating content with ChatGPT, plagiarism is a legal risk. Since the AI model can mimic human writing so well, it may produce content that unwittingly plagiarizes or paraphrases another work without giving due credit to the original creator. Because of this, the individual or company using ChatGPT-created content may face charges of plagiarism, which can be detrimental to their reputation.

Users must critically and responsibly assess AI-generated content to verify legal and ethical compliance. Furthermore, it is necessary to build a legal framework that tackles the particular issues given by AI-generated material by encouraging interaction between stakeholders such as legislators, AI developers, and content providers. The possible legal concerns associated with using ChatGPT can be reduced if users work together to set clear rules and best practices.

Human Touch

The lack of human touch and customization in the AI-generated output is one of the obstacles that users experience. AI language models such as ChatGPT can be extremely effective and efficient when it comes to the generation of content; nevertheless, this is also one of the obstacles that users face. ChatGPT can help you get more done in less time, but it may miss some of the subtleties, emotions, and unique voices that make writing worth reading and remembering.

The artificial intelligence model in ChatGPT has some trouble understanding and conveying the nuanced emotions, complexities, and cultural references that are characteristic of human writing. The AI model may be able to imitate human language patterns, but it can't understand or empathize with its readers the way humans can, which prevents them from writing content that truly connects with people. Because of this, AI-generated material may end up being factually correct yet fail to emotionally connect with or engage the intended audience.

The difficulty of adding a human touch comes up again in the form of customization. Human authors have the distinct advantage of being able to cater their work to the interests, demographics, and life experiences of their readers. ChatGPT, on the other hand, can find it difficult to reach the same degree of customization and personalization because it creates content based on patterns discovered through a massive volume of text data, which might not always match the distinctive qualities of a particular audience.

The human touch problem also affects the imaginative side of writing. ChatGPT can produce content that makes sense and is free of grammatical errors, but it may lack the originality, inventiveness, and ingenuity of human writers. It may be challenging for an AI model like ChatGPT to recreate the unique, insightful, and engaging content that human writers can produce by drawing on their own experiences, opinions, and creativity.

Humanizing ChatGPT requires that users view AI-generated information as a resource that can supplement, rather than eliminate, human writing. Writers can use ChatGPT to develop first drafts or ideas, then refine and personalize the text with their distinctive voice and perspective.

Chapter 4

The Process of Using ChatGPT

ChatGPT's implementation is critical to realizing the model's full capability in contexts ranging from content production to customer service. This chapter offers helpful advice on how to use ChatGPT efficiently, including how to interact with the model step-by-step, examples of input prompts that produce the appropriate output, and suggestions for choosing and modifying output options. By learning and mastering these methods, users may maximize the efficiency, quality, and relevance of AI-generated content and get the most out of ChatGPT.

Determining the Task

To begin efficiently utilizing ChatGPT, one must first choose the precise activity or application that will make use of the AI language model. Content creation can include everything from writing articles or social media postings to creating chatbots for customer care or providing translation services to break down language barriers. The user's ability to determine the intended task is crucial since it allows them to choose the optimal implementation of ChatGPT, as well as the relevant training data and prompts.

Selecting the appropriate ChatGPT model is vital since each variant serves a unique function and has unique features. Some implementations may be better suited to chatbot creation conversational encounters, while others may be better suited to content generation. In order to get the most out of the AI-generated output, users should pick the version that is most applicable to the work at hand.

Choosing the right version of ChatGPT is only half the battle; figuring out what kind of training data will be needed is just as important. The effectiveness of an AI model is greatly affected by the quality of the training data it uses to learn linguistic patterns and structures. To ensure that the material generated by ChatGPT is in line with the expectations and preferences of its intended audience, it is crucial to give the platform accurate and relevant training data from the domain of interest.

Last but not least, defining the task requires creating suitable prompts that direct ChatGPT to produce the correct output. The usefulness and accuracy of computer-generated information can be greatly improved with a carefully crafted prompt. If the user wants to write a blog post, for instance, they should give a detailed prompt outlining the topic, the structure they want, and any other criteria or limits. In this way, customers can instruct ChatGPT to generate material that more closely meets their requirements.

Selecting the Appropriate Version of ChatGPT

Since there are a number of various versions of ChatGPT, each with its own set of capabilities and restrictions, it is important to pick the one that is best suited to the task at hand and the needs of the end user. Several variables enter into the decision-making process, including the complexity of the model, the reliability of the available training data, and the qualities of the model that are essential to the goal at hand.

The model's computing needs and performance are strongly affected by the model's size. For tasks with restricted hardware resources or real-time applications, smaller models are preferable since they are faster and use fewer computational resources. Larger models, however, tend to perform better because they can produce more consistent, accurate, and context-aware results. ChatGPT users should weigh their individual needs against the system's performance and resource limits when deciding which version is best for them.

The standard of the data used for training is an additional factor to think about. A ChatGPT model's accuracy is proportional to the quality of its training data. It is essential for producing accurate and trustworthy results that the selected version has been trained on high-quality, diversified, and objective data. A version trained on a large dataset related to their domain or sector is more likely to provide material that suits their needs.

Finally, it's up to users to think about which aspects of the ChatGPT model are essential to accomplishing their goals. It's possible to find variants of ChatGPT that perform better than others when used for specific tasks like writing, talking to others, translating, or even generating code. These domain-specific models may offer improved performance since they incorporate optimizations based on data collected from that specific domain. One version may be better suited to chatbot creation than another since it places greater emphasis on delivering timely, coherent responses that are also acceptable in context.

Here are a few examples illustrating how determining the task can help users effectively utilize ChatGPT:

Example 1: Content Creation for a Health Blog

Task: Generate a blog post about the benefits of a plant-based diet.

Version: A ChatGPT version tailored for content generation.

Training Data: Provide articles and research papers related to plant-based diets and nutrition.

Prompt: "Write a 1,000-word informative blog post discussing the top five health benefits of a plant-based diet, supported by scientific evidence."

Example 2: Chatbot Development for Customer Support

Task: Create a chatbot for an e-commerce website to handle customer inquiries.

Version: A ChatGPT version optimized for conversational interactions.

Training Data: Provide chat logs from previous customer support interactions, FAQs, and product information.

Prompt: Users can provide context for the chatbot, such as "You are a customer support chatbot for XYZ online store. Help the customer with their inquiry."

Example 3: Translation Services

Task: Translate English text into Spanish for a travel website.

Version: A ChatGPT version designed for language translation.

Training Data: Provide bilingual text data from travel websites, articles, and guides in both English and Spanish.

Prompt: "Translate the following English text into Spanish: 'Discover the top 10 must-see attractions in Paris, including the Eiffel Tower, Louvre Museum, and Notre-Dame Cathedral.'"

By clearly defining the tasks and providing appropriate versions, training data, and prompts, users can effectively guide ChatGPT to generate high-quality output that meets their specific needs and requirements across various applications.

Preparing the Data and Prompts

To make efficient use of ChatGPT, it is necessary to provide the user with high-quality training data as well as prompts that are tailored to the specific activity being performed by the user. It is crucial to methodically prepare the data and prompts, as the quality of input strongly determines the resultant output.

Social networking sites, news stories, scholarly journals, and company databases are just some of the places where information can be gathered during the data collection process. In order for the model to produce accurate and relevant results, it must be fed a large amount of relevant data from the target domain.

In order to get ready, you need to clean the data. The accuracy of the model could be negatively affected by noise, inconsistencies, or biases present in the raw data. Users should spend effort weeding out irrelevant information and checking that what's left is reliable, objective, and consistent with preferences.

The ability to provide useful prompts is a crucial part of using ChatGPT. The model takes prompts as input and uses them to generate answers. They need to be understandable, brief, and task oriented. It's important to give the model enough information in the prompt so that it can fully grasp the user's needs and provide a suitable response.

For instance, "Write an informative and engaging blog post about the importance of sustainable fashion, discussing its benefits, industry trends, and ways for consumers to make more eco-friendly choices" is a good prompt for an assignment that requires generating a blog post about sustainable fashion.

Users can learn the most efficient prompt structure for a given activity by experimenting with several prompt styles and modifying them depending on the model's output. To help the model produce the required results, it may be useful to include open-ended questions, specific instructions, or limits on the response structure.

Access ChatGPT

As soon as the data and prompts are ready, ChatGPT can be accessed via many different platforms and tools. ChatGPT can be accessed either by the OpenAI API or the Hugging Face transformers library.

The OpenAI API is a popular system that facilitates user-to-user communication over ChatGPT. In order to utilize this API, users must first register for an API key on the OpenAI website. The API key enables users to begin utilizing ChatGPT for their defined purposes once it is integrated into their apps. The API is often accompanied by comprehensive documentation and code samples to aid with the integration process.

Another well-liked option for getting at ChatGPT is the Hugging Face Transformers library. Among the several pre-trained models available in this open-source package is ChatGPT. Users can import the required modules into their Python environment after Hugging Face's transformers library has been installed. Similar to the OpenAI API, some models may require an access token before they can be interacted with.

After logging into ChatGPT from their preferred platform, users can start producing content with the provided data and instructions. Users can get customized results by feeding the model their responses to the model's cues. The resulting output must be closely monitored, and the prompts or model settings must be adjusted as needed for the best outcomes. To get the appropriate results, users may need to try out a number of different configurations and prompt formats.

Fine-Tuning ChatGPT

In order to enhance the accuracy and relevance of the generated content, fine-tuning ChatGPT models for specific tasks and applications is a crucial step. By customizing the model according to the user's requirements, it becomes more effective in producing suitable outputs. There are several approaches to fine-tuning, which include providing additional training data, adjusting hyperparameters, and employing transfer learning techniques.

Providing additional training data: To fine-tune ChatGPT, users can supplement the pre-existing training data with additional domain-specific data. This helps the model become more familiar with the specific context, vocabulary, and style relevant to the task. The additional data should be carefully selected, cleaned, and processed before being used for fine-tuning.

Adjusting hyperparameters: Another aspect of fine-tuning involves tweaking the model's hyperparameters, such as learning rate, batch size, and the number of training epochs. By adjusting these parameters, users can optimize the model's performance and tailor it to the specific task. It is essential to experiment with different hyperparameter values and monitor the model's performance to find the optimal configuration.

Using transfer learning techniques: Transfer learning is a powerful technique in which a pre-trained model is further trained on a new dataset to improve its performance in a specific domain. By leveraging the knowledge gained from pre-training, ChatGPT can quickly adapt to new tasks with minimal additional training. This approach is particularly useful when dealing with limited data or highly specialized domains.

Fine-tuning ChatGPT requires expertise in machine learning and natural language processing. However, there are tools and tutorials available to assist users in this process. Resources such as OpenAI's fine-tuning guide and Hugging Face's transformers library offer valuable guidance for users looking to customize ChatGPT for their specific needs. Through fine-tuning, users can significantly enhance the performance of ChatGPT, ensuring that it generates outputs that are accurate, relevant, and tailored to the specific task at hand.

Reviewing and Editing the Output

Users must check and edit the output of ChatGPT thoroughly to ensure it is accurate, relevant, and maintains the intended quality or tone. Text written by AI may seem and sound human, but it could still have typos, inconsistencies, or be missing crucial context.

Making minor adjustments: Sometimes, the output generated by ChatGPT simply needs slight modifications. Making small aesthetic adjustments to bring the text in line with the desired tone may include fixing grammatical or punctuation mistakes, rephrasing uncomfortable lines, or something similar. By making these changes, the output can be improved upon and made more coherent and easier to understand.

Reworking the content: If the final product lacks the expected level of quality, tone, or relevancy, it may be required to rework the content in its entirety. When this happens, users need to point out where ChatGPT is falling short and give it fresh input prompts to help it produce better results. This cycle can be performed as many times as necessary to produce a result that is up to snuff.

Ensuring credibility and reputation: For the sake of credibility and reputation, it is crucial that the AI-generated content be reviewed and edited thoroughly before being released into the wild. The material supplied should be correct, well-organized, and in line with the needs of the intended audience. This is especially crucial in areas where trust and reputation are essential, such as news, academia, and professional writing.

Chapter 5

How to Use ChatGPT for Writing

ChatGPT's flexibility makes it useful for a wide variety of writing projects. For example, writers may struggle during the brainstorming phase to come up with original ideas or the right slant for their story. By responding to the user's input with a wide variety of recommendations and viewpoints, ChatGPT can spark creativity and speed up the brainstorming process. Overcoming barriers and laying the groundwork for an engaging piece can be aided by this.

The same holds true for outlining, where ChatGPT can facilitate the arrangement of ideas into a logical framework for the author. ChatGPT is helpful since it can provide a framework for their ideas or suggest an order that makes sense. This frees them up to concentrate on crafting compelling and instructive pieces of writing.

Editing is an essential part of writing since it helps to refine the text and make it more comprehensible and consistent. Content written using ChatGPT may occasionally need to be rephrased or reworked, but the tool may help writers out by giving alternative sentence patterns, pointing out grammar or punctuation issues, and suggesting stylistic enhancements.

Throughout this chapter, readers will discover various techniques and strategies to maximize the benefits of ChatGPT in the writing process.

Improving Writing Efficiency

ChatGPT has the ability to greatly improve productivity and speed up the creative process when used for writing jobs. Content creators, emailers, social media posters, chatbot programmers, and translators can all benefit from using this sophisticated language model to produce higher-quality work in less time.

It is essential to define the precise writing-related job or application prior to implementing ChatGPT. This makes it so that users can fine-tune their strategies to make the most of ChatGPT and improve their writing. Users can select the best version of ChatGPT for their needs and have a better understanding of the training data and prompts needed to generate the desired content by defining the work at hand.

For instance, ChatGPT can be used to generate material like articles, blog entries, and product descriptions with minimum human input. Writers may get AI to produce well-structured content that can be readily updated and adjusted to match their specific needs by providing relevant prompts and context. This not only fosters more constant content output but also speeds up the writing process by helping overcome writer's block.

ChatGPT can help you write emails that are polished, to the point, and easy to read. Users may ensure that their emails are effective and interesting by providing the model with the major arguments and the desired tone and then receiving suggestions for phrasing. Those who have trouble putting their thoughts into words on paper may find this useful, as may those who have to deal with a lot of emails.

ChatGPT can be used in the world of social media to make postings that stand out and connect with the intended audience. Users can create interesting, relevant, and targeted social media content by learning about the network and their audience's demographics. This can make it easier for people to keep up an engaging social media presence with minimal investment of time and energy.

In addition to its usage in translation and the creation of chatbots, ChatGPT improves the user experience and opens up new channels of contact. Users are able to develop chatbots that either translate material in a way that is seamless between languages or that deliver informative responses that sound natural by training the model on multilingual datasets or conversational data.

Digital Marketing

ChatGPT stands out as a game-changing platform for digital marketers thanks to its ability to produce persuasive content that actively involves and converts the intended audience. Marketers may increase the efficacy and reach of their campaigns by using ChatGPT for a variety of marketing tasks.

ChatGPT is particularly useful for writing attention-grabbing advertisements and product descriptions. Marketers can receive high-quality content that emphasizes the benefits of their products or services by giving the AI model information about the demographics of their target audience. This not only helps you save time but also guarantees that the content generated will reflect your brand's tone and will be appealing to your target audience.

As an added bonus, ChatGPT may be used to streamline the process of coming up with material for online platforms like social media and blogs. ChatGPT provides marketers with a wealth of ideas for material to write about, increasing the likelihood that their messages will be read and shared. This not only increases productivity but also guarantees that the content created is current and interesting to the intended audience.

ChatGPT's ability to tailor digital marketing campaigns to individual users is another strength. ChatGPT may generate personalized marketing messages by evaluating user behavior and preferences. As a result of this increased individualization, marketing campaigns are more likely to resonate with their target audience, resulting in more conversions and stronger customer loyalty. As a result, targeted marketing communications have the potential to boost click-through and conversion rates.

Furthermore, ChatGPT's insightful data and helpful recommendations can aid in improving marketing outcomes. ChatGPT provides data-driven advice to improve marketing tactics by analyzing campaign performance and recommending areas for improvement. This can lead to more efficient campaigns, which in turn can improve marketing results and ROI.

Fiction and Non-Fiction Writing

ChatGPT's advanced features are especially useful for both creative and academic writing, as the AI-driven tool may accelerate the writing process and free up writers to focus on polishing their work. Writers of all stripes have found ChatGPT useful for everything from brainstorming story ideas and developing characters to summarizing articles and conducting research.

Fiction Writing

ChatGPT can be used to generate many different aspects of fictional writing, such as story, character, setting, and dialogue. Authors can obtain imaginative recommendations to expand upon or fine-tune their stories after submitting pertinent information to the AI model, such as genre, setting, or major characters. As a result, you may rest assured that the finished product will be both efficient and interesting.

ChatGPT can also be used to produce discussion prompts and ideas, adding much-needed originality and inspiration to the writing process. Writers are freed up to focus on the story's tempo, tone, and structure because the AI model can generate useful and relevant, and natural-sounding language by assessing the context and characters.

Non-Fiction Writing

Writing for academic purposes (reports, essays, etc.) is another area where ChatGPT might be useful. The AI model can assist writers by developing ideas and performing research, allowing for the examination of diverse perspectives, the collection of pertinent data, and the synthesis of knowledge that ultimately results in a work that is both complete and well-informed. This not only shortens the time it takes to do research but also increases confidence in the reliability, applicability, and insight of the findings.

ChatGPT can also be used to summarize articles or news briefs, helping writers simplify difficult content. Writers can get a condensed version that emphasizes the most salient arguments, statistics, and conclusions by feeding them into an AI model. This feature is invaluable for journalists, academics, and content providers who must swiftly and clearly relay information to their readers or viewers.

Academic Writing

Students, scholars, and professionals in a wide range of professions all benefit from developing their academic writing skills. It frequently calls for pinpoint accuracy, well-organized thought, and articulate explanation of complex concepts. ChatGPT can be a huge help in many ways for academic writing, improving both efficiency and quality.

ChatGPT can be useful in many ways, one of which is by helping to spark new ideas and increase productivity while writing. AI can help authors organize their ideas and create a logical framework for their writing by offering suggestions and prompts. As an added bonus, ChatGPT can help automate tedious processes like citation formatting, allowing you to focus on the more important components of your paper.

ChatGPT's capacity to aid with research, data analysis, and the creation of tables and figures is another significant application in academic writing. ChatGPT's ability to analyze massive datasets and synthesize information from multiple sources enables authors to produce in-depth academic articles and reports that include appropriate visual representations.

ChatGPT's language features are useful for non-native English speakers who have trouble writing in academic English. Non-native speakers will have an easier time expressing themselves because the AI can offer suggestions for proper terminology, syntax, and sentence structure.

In addition to pointing out blank spots in the literature, ChatGPT can advise authors on how to delve deeper into under-researched subfields. The overall worth and impact of academic work can be greatly increased by the capacity to spot gaps and give relevant recommendations.

Last but not least, ChatGPT can serve as a helpful instrument for editing and proofreading. ChatGPT may assist in making sure the final product is up to the rigorous standards of academic writing by checking it for mistakes, inconsistencies, and places where improvement is needed. Correcting grammar, making sure sources are cited correctly, and making the text easier to read are all part of this process.

Chapter 6

Humanizing AI-Generated Content

The subject of content creation has seen major advancements as a result of the rapidly advancing technology of artificial intelligence. ChatGPT and other models of artificial intelligence language can now generate text with a quality comparable to that of a human. Yet, producing material that is generated by AI that sounds authentic and natural is not an easy task. In order to assist in the resolution of this issue, the chapter titled "Humanizing AI-Generated Content" provides recommendations on how to make the output of ChatGPT sound more natural and conversational.

It is essential to give the content generated by AI a human touch. Before artificial intelligence-generated content can maintain its credibility and inspire meaningful connections, it must first be comprehended by the audience for which it was created. In this chapter, we will address the significance of adding a human element to content that has been generated by AI, as well as the potential impact that this has on the effectiveness of communication.

This chapter will present various strategies for humanizing AI-generated content in order to assist readers in acquiring a more human touch. Readers will come away with a comprehensive comprehension of the numerous approaches that may be taken to humanize AI-generated content. These approaches range from modifying the text's style and structure to including elements of storytelling and personalizing.

The Importance of Humanizing AI-Generated Content

How we produce and consume data has been revolutionized by the widespread use of information provided by artificial intelligence. Humanizing AI-generated content is becoming increasingly crucial to keep it interesting, timely, and meaningful to the intended audience as its use grows. The gap between artificial intelligence-generated output and genuine human communication can be closed by humanizing content created by authors and content providers.

First of all, keeping readers interested in AI-generated content requires humanizing it. Genuine and personable writing is more likely to attract readers than impersonal or generic pieces. Content creators may pique their audience's interest and get them to read, share, and interact with AI-generated content by adding a human touch.

Second, adding a human touch to information can keep it from sounding robotic or generic. Despite tremendous progress in this area in recent years, AI-generated material can still sometimes fail to capture the complexity, perspective, and emotional intelligence of human communication. This may lead to writing that comes out as cold, indifferent, or even offensive to the target audience. Creators can improve the authenticity and appeal of AI-generated material by adding human touches.

Lastly, by adding a human touch, AI-generated content becomes more accessible, interesting, and effective. In order to make AI-generated content more relatable, it is common practice to add touches of individualization, emotional resonance, and narrative. These additions can make the reading experience more vivid and memorable for the audience, which in turn increases the content's effectiveness. As a result, content creators may see an uptick in positive measures like user happiness and engagement.

Techniques for Humanizing AI-Generated Content

Humanizing AI's output is crucial to keeping it interesting and relevant to its intended audience as this type of content becomes more commonplace. Many methods exist for giving AI-generated content a more human feel and making it more readable and engaging.

Adding Individuality and Humor

Including the author's voice and a sense of humor is a great way to inject humanity into AI-generated content. Content providers can make their writing stand out and more interesting to the reader by adopting a distinctive voice, tone, or style. In particular, humor may be a powerful means of establishing a personal rapport with readers by creating a sense of familiarity and mutual understanding. Puns, wordplay, and humorous anecdotes can help you attain this goal.

Including Storytelling Elements

Storytelling elements are another way to give AI-generated content a more human feel. To do this, the content may require the addition of characterization, story structure, or dramatic turns. Storytelling approaches allow content makers to capitalize on the universal appeal of narrative to make their work more engaging and memorable. Telling a tale about a company or product you're trying to sell is a great way to get people invested in your content and your business. The use of narrative arcs, conflict, and resolution, as well as the introduction of likable characters and events, are all good ways to put this strategy into practice.

Integrating Cultural References and Idioms

The use of colloquial language or cultural references that are meaningful to the intended audience is a third method for humanizing AI-generated material. Using catchphrases and common references helps writers connect with their audience on an emotional level. This can help to develop a more genuine and approachable tone, which is especially useful when writing for a targeted demographic or geographic readership. Learn the idioms, slang, and cultural references that will resonate with your audience, and work them into the text where they make sense.

Balancing Accuracy and Creativity

Creating entertaining and useful AI-generated content requires balancing accuracy and originality. Striking this equilibrium calls for a methodical approach to editing and revision to fulfill the needs of the intended readers while also creating something fresh and engaging for them to read.

Achieving an Ideal Level of Accuracy

Accuracy must be prioritized if AI-generated material is to retain its credibility and reliability. This includes double-checking all of the numbers and making sure everything makes sense and is organized properly. Also, it is crucial to refrain from embellishment or distortion, both of which might cast doubt on the veracity of the data supplied. When adding a personal touch to content, it's important to keep in mind that inaccuracies or biases in the source material can detract from the final product.

Infusing Creativity

Although precision is essential, it is equally important that information generated by AI be interesting and pleasurable to read. To do this, the work must be infused with creativity, such as through the use of evocative language, captivating storytelling, and fresh points of view. Consider modifying the style, tone, or voice of the text to make it more relatable and appropriate for the intended audience or function. The topic can be made more interesting and approachable by trying out a variety of rhetorical strategies, such as the use of metaphors, similes, and tales.

Facilitating a Better Reading Experience

To make the AI-generated content more interesting to read, it could be helpful to include some sort of context or background information. This can be done through the use of appropriate anecdotes, cultural insights, or concrete instances from the past or present. By expanding the reader's knowledge and perspective, the author increases the likelihood that the reader will be interested in and inspired by the work. You could also think about including visuals like pictures, graphs, and charts to enhance the reading experience.

The Role of Tone and Voice

Humanizing AI-generated content requires paying close attention to tone and voice. The writer will feel more at ease with the content if the tone and voice are clearly established. This will make the content seem more relevant and personal. In this section, we'll discuss the role that tone, and voice play in making AI-generated material more approachable, as well as offer some suggestions for doing so.

First and foremost, your voice and tone are essential to connecting with your reader. AI-generated content can increase trust and comprehension by adopting a tone and voice that is familiar to the intended readers. For a blog post aimed at a younger readership, for instance, using a more casual, conversational tone can make the text more relevant, while for a professional or academic audience, a more formal tone might be appropriate.

The second way to make content more accessible and interesting is to use language and style that resonate with the intended readers. Content creators benefit from knowing their target demographic inside and out so they can produce material that speaks directly to their interests and values. A customer service chatbot, for instance, might benefit from an upbeat and positive tone, whereas a policy paper or legal document could call for a more authoritative one.

The tone and voice used in communications can play an important part in representing the brand or company. Maintaining a constant persona and message across all of your organization's channels will assist in creating a reliable and trustworthy brand impression. A corporation concerned with environmental issues can utilize a tone that is both educational and impassioned.

Ethical Considerations of Content Generation

Humanizing AI-generated material requires thinking about ethical implications. It is critical to recognize and solve the ethical problems involved with content generation as the use of AI-generated material grows more widespread. We will examine the ethical aspects of humanizing AI-generated content in this section, concentrating on topics such as bias, confidentiality, and intellectual property, as well as providing recommendations for responsible content creation.

Humanizing AI-generated content raises a number of important ethical considerations, one of the most prominent of which is the possibility of bias. Massive volumes of data are used to train AI models like ChatGPT, and this data may reflect biases that exist in the actual world. This means that the models' conclusions may unintentionally reinforce or intensify existing biases. Creators of AI-generated material should be aware of this problem and take measures to detect and correct any biases they may find. The use of many data sources, specific guidelines for the AI model, and a thorough examination of the results for bias are all possible steps in this direction.

Second, it's crucial to check that no deceptive or misleading methods are used when humanizing AI-generated content. Avoiding dishonest practices such as information fabrication, plagiarism, and so on is essential to maintaining the integrity of one's work and protecting one's reputation. Ethical content production requires authors to check the precision of data produced by AI models and provide due credit where credit is due.

Humanizing AI-generated material also raises important privacy concerns. Creators of content have a responsibility to protect users' privacy by not sharing or exploiting any personally identifiable information without first obtaining appropriate permission. Using people's real-life experiences or stories without their consent could, for example, violate their privacy or cause them harm. To reduce the likelihood of this happening, creators should remove or obscure any identifying information before including it in their works.

Finally, when adding personality to AI-generated content, it's important to think about IP issues. It is crucial to check if the AI-generated content violates any copyrights or trademarks. Artists should be familiar with intellectual property regulations and follow them, whether that means relying only on their own ideas or giving correct credit when credit is due.

Chapter 7

Improving Productivity With ChatGPT

Writers and other content creators in today's fast-paced environment are always looking to increase output and streamline processes. ChatGPT is one tool that has evolved as a result of the development of AI to help writers save time, enhance productivity, and eliminate tedious, repetitive writing duties. This chapter digs into the nuts and bolts of using ChatGPT and shows how it can improve the writing process in general.

In the first part of the chapter, we look at how ChatGPT might help authors become more productive by suggesting relevant content, reducing the amount of time spent on mundane activities, and freeing up mental space for more in-depth, strategic thinking. It then goes on to talk about how content creators can use ChatGPT to assist them in coming up with ideas and overcoming writer's block by using AI-generated prompts and suggestions.

The chapter then delves into the use of ChatGPT for research and fact-checking, demonstrating how the AI model may be put to work to efficiently and rapidly amass data without compromising quality. In addition to being a time-saver, the resultant text will be of a higher standard.

The chapter concludes with a discussion of how writers might make the most of ChatGPT's features to streamline their writing processes. ChatGPT is a useful tool for writers because it helps them with everything from brainstorming to outlining to drafting to offering feedback and suggestions for development.

By the end of this chapter, readers will have a firm grasp on how to make the most of ChatGPT to improve their writing workflow and, in turn, their productivity.

How ChatGPT Can Improve Productivity

ChatGPT's ability to automate routine writing processes, speed up the production of high-quality content, and protect writers from burnout makes it a valuable addition to any writer's workflow. Here, we investigate what role ChatGPT can play in bringing forth these enhancements.

According to research conducted by MIT, corporate AI teams who make use of ChatGPT 4.0 services achieve higher levels of efficiency and success in their work assignments than teams that do not exist. Companies need to make sure that their primary vendors use Generative AI technology to implement more robust and up-to-date AI customer service models (Noy and Zhang, 2023).

Let's dive deep into how ChatGPT has come to our rescue.

Automating Routine Writing Tasks

Blog posts, social media updates, and email replies are just some of the many forms of written communication that may be automated with the help of ChatGPT. By having these mundane processes automated, writers are freed up to concentrate on the planning and innovation that make their work so compelling. Productivity may rise when workers reallocate the time they would have spent writing by hand to more valuable endeavors.

Producing High-Quality Work With Minimal Effort and Time Investment

ChatGPT's capacity to generate high-quality content with minimum input from the writer is a major benefit. Writers who are pressed for time or have a lot of work to do can benefit from the AI model's ability to generate intelligible, well-structured writing. By making use of ChatGPT, authors can cut down on wasted effort and concentrate on other aspects of their work.

Getting Past Writer's Block

The inability to write can be a frustrating and time-consuming problem. ChatGPT provides writers with a variety of ideas and solutions to help them break through their blocks. Increased productivity can be achieved by the use of AI-generated prompts, blueprints, or even entire drafts to help writers overcome writer's block and keep a steady flow of work.

Preventing Burnout and Increasing Output

It takes a lot of mental and emotional energy to write. If a writer doesn't take enough breaks between projects, burnout can set in and significantly reduce their output. By automating mundane activities and creating fresh ideas, ChatGPT can relieve some of the stress that comes with content creation so that writers can take a breather and get back to work refreshed. Increased output and a more manageable writing routine may result from this.

Using ChatGPT for Content Ideation and Brainstorming

Writers' workflows can be completely transformed by integrating ChatGPT into the process of content ideation and brainstorming. The AI resource can be used to produce ideas and inspiration, offer prompts or jumping-off places, and the present novel takes on a wide range of themes. Here, we'll look at why utilizing ChatGPT to generate ideas and brainstorm is so helpful.

Generating Inspiration and Ideas

Finding new angles from which to approach their writing is a constant struggle for authors. With the help of ChatGPT, writers can get a wide range of ideas and suggestions on their selected topic. The AI model may analyze the input prompt and generate pertinent suggestions, which can help to jumpstart the creative process and present a variety of possible avenues for the writer to investigate.

Providing Ideas or Starting Points

In order to get through the dreaded writer's block and get back to work, sometimes all you need is a springboard. ChatGPT is great for coming up with ideas or prompts that can be used as a jumping-off point for writing or brainstorming. By providing the AI model with a broad, overarching stimulus, authors can obtain a variety of ideas that may serve as jumping-off points for their writing or point them in the direction of the most interesting angle to explore.

Bringing Fresh Viewpoints and Approaches

Because of its powerful processing capabilities, ChatGPT can come up with fresh takes on a wide range of issues. By tapping into the AI model's vast store of information, authors gain access to perspectives and ideas they might not have explored before. This not only improves the quality of the content but also makes it stand out from other works in the same vein.

Improving Teamwork and Brainstorming

Group brainstorming sessions can also benefit from using ChatGPT. The AI model's ability to provide a wide range of proposals can spark debate and discussion among team members, ultimately leading to the creation of more polished and original material. By facilitating communication and teamwork, ChatGPT boosts the effectiveness of brainstorming sessions.

Using ChatGPT for Research and Fact-Checking

ChatGPT may be a huge time-saver and quality booster when it comes to doing research and reviewing facts before writing. ChatGPT's ability to provide timely and relevant data to authors will allow them to produce higher-quality, more precise content. This section examines the advantages of utilizing ChatGPT for fact-checking and research.

Conducting Research

ChatGPT is able to do this thanks to its huge knowledge base, which it has constructed through the analysis of massive volumes of data.

ChatGPT allows authors to quickly and easily do research by entering relevant prompts or queries and receiving answers based on the AI model's expertise. In addition to being a time- and labor-saver, this also guarantees that the data presented is correct and up to date, which raises the content's quality generally.

Fact-Checking

Maintaining trust and reliability among readers relies heavily on the precision of written content. Writers can utilize ChatGPT to confirm facts with minimal effort and time investment. Writers can get the AI model's validation or explanation on particular content-related questions or prompts, bolstering the credibility and accuracy of their writing.

Providing Solutions to Frequent Problems

Writers frequently require information that addresses frequently asked questions or concerns about their chosen topic. ChatGPT can rapidly generate answers to these queries, equipping authors with the data they need to produce work that is both useful and accurate. By automating this step, ChatGPT frees up the writer's time to concentrate on other areas of the project, including creating a compelling story or strengthening their arguments.

Facilitating More Efficient Research

Finding the information you need via conventional methods of research can be a time-consuming and tiresome process. By giving authors instantaneous access to important and reliable material, ChatGPT facilitates a more streamlined research process. Finding and verifying material takes less time and effort when using this method, freeing up more time for authors to concentrate on producing superior content.

Streamlining the Writing Process With ChatGPT

When ChatGPT is used during the writing process, productivity and organization are both improved. ChatGPT helps authors produce high-quality content quickly and effortlessly by automating typical writing processes and providing assistance with many elements of content development. Let's look at how implementing ChatGPT into your writing workflow may do wonders for your efficiency and output.

Creating High-Quality Content

The sophisticated language model used by ChatGPT allows for the generation of excellent, thought-provoking writing. Writers are able to produce well-organized and logical work that is consistent with the required topic and tone with very little guidance. This allows authors to produce content faster and concentrate on tailoring the final product to their needs.

Improve Your Writing Fluency and Precision

By offering suggestions, ideas, and even full phrases depending on the input, ChatGPT can help authors boost their productivity. This helps authors get beyond writer's block, keeps them on track, and cuts down on typos. This means that writers can increase their output while decreasing their workload.

Helping With Revisions and Edits

Editing and proofreading are two other areas where ChatGPT can be put to use. ChatGPT helps writers improve their drafts by suggesting ways to reorganize sentences, fix grammar, and expand their vocabulary. In addition to reducing production time, this also improves the quality of the finished product.

Generating Relevant Content

ChatGPT enables authors to modify their writing for a particular readership or function. Writers can develop content that is suitable for a wide range of purposes by modifying the input prompts, including official reports, conversational blog entries, and persuasive marketing materials. Because of this leeway, authors can quickly and easily develop a wide variety of content types.

Chapter 8

ChatGPT for Efficient Income Strategies

To survive and thrive in today's competitive digital market, it's crucial to find innovative ways to generate revenue. In this chapter, we'll look at how you can utilize ChatGPT, a robust AI language model, to make money from writing jobs, including article writing, copywriting, and ghostwriting. Readers can maximize their earnings by utilizing the features of ChatGPT to have access to simpler income strategies.

ChatGPT's entry into the writing industry has radically altered the process of content production, giving writers more ways to earn money for their efforts. Writers and business owners alike have grown to rely on ChatGPT because of its flexibility and ability to produce high-quality, engaging material across a wide variety of topics and formats.

In this chapter, we'll look into the various ways you can make money with ChatGPT. We'll go through strategies for making money off of ChatGPT content and show you how to put them into practice.

Overview of Income Opportunities With ChatGPT

ChatGPT's expanding features have made it possible for more people and businesses to make money off of the platform. Products and services for many different sectors and industries can be developed with the help of AI-generated content. Here are some ways to make money with ChatGPT that we will go through in detail.

Blogs, Websites, and Social Media Platforms

A steady stream of high-quality content that can be monetized through advertising or affiliate marketing can be generated by ChatGPT and used on blogs, websites, and social networking platforms. Attracting advertisers and affiliate partners that are prepared to pay for access to your readers is a lot easier when you have an engaged and interested audience.

E-Books, Courses, and Digital Products

You can use ChatGPT to make digital items like books, courses, and more to sell online. You can use the AI's capacity to produce interesting and useful content to your advantage by developing specialty or industry-specific goods with higher added value. These digital items have the potential to provide substantial passive revenue if properly marketed.

Customer Support and Services

Use ChatGPT to assist customers with issues or sell further products. By charging clients on an hourly or project basis for AI-assisted content development, you may earn a steady money stream while simultaneously saving time and effort. Freelance writers, copywriters, and consultants who are trying to maximize their billable hours may find this particularly helpful.

Market Research and Analysis

Businesses and organizations can use ChatGPT for market research and analysis. You can establish yourself as an invaluable asset to businesses that are looking to better understand their market and uncover growth prospects by delivering accurate and timely information. Consulting, report writing, and similar services might become a valuable source of income as a result.

Personalized Content Creation

It is possible to make money off of the personalized content generated by ChatGPT by selling things like resumes, cover letters, and marketing collateral. You can establish yourself as an industry expert and command higher rates by customizing your content to individual customer's demands.

Chatbots and Virtual Assistants

Get money by selling chatbots or virtual assistants you make with

Chat Bot to businesses for use in customer service or other areas. You may create a useful tool that improves productivity and simplifies interactions with customers by having the AI produce responses and insights.

Podcasts and Video Channels

Podcasts and video channels can use ChatGPT to generate content that can be monetized through advertising and sponsorship deals. Consistent, interesting content provided by AI can help you build a loyal following and find support from businesses looking to advertise or fund your work.

Chat-Based Games and Quizzes

Make use of ChatGPT to make quizzes and other chat-based games that can be monetized with in-app purchases and advertising. Offering in-app purchases of more content or ad space is one way to monetize a game or quiz that provides users with a fun and engaging experience.

New Business or Product Ideas

Utilize ChatGPT to think of innovative business and product ideas that can be developed into profitable businesses. Discovering fresh ideas and openings allows you to carve out a niche in the market and lay the groundwork for a prosperous enterprise.

Data Trend Identification and Consulting

Data analysis using ChatGPT can be used to discover patterns that can then be turned into consulting or other revenue streams. With the insights offered by AI, you can give your customers what they need to make better decisions and fine-tune their approaches.

Social Media Management

Get more attention online by offering your services to other people or businesses by using ChatGPT to create interesting posts for their social media pages. Helping clients expand their fan bases and raise awareness of their brands through regular, high-quality content creation can lead to a stable stream of money from social media management services.

Content Curation

Use ChatGPT to compile articles about a single subject for a newsletter or niche website. To earn income from advertising, partnerships, or premium content offers, you need a dedicated audience who eagerly awaits your updates. AI-generated content can help you find this audience.

Copywriting Services

Employ ChatGPT to write sales text, including product details, sales letters, and landing sites, which converts. Using AI-generated content to develop persuasive copy that converts can help you establish credibility as a skilled writer and land big contracts and continuous business.

Ghostwriting

If you need help with writing projects but would rather not have your name attached to any of the text, consider using ChatGPT as a ghostwriter. You can turn a profit as a ghostwriter since clients will pay more for your services because of the value you add due to your knowledge and confidentiality.

Translation and Localization Services

Make use of ChatGPT's built-in translation and localization tools to help organizations and individuals reach new international audiences with their content. There is a rising need for material in several languages, and you can capitalize on this by offering translation and localization services that are both accurate and sensitive to target audiences' cultural backgrounds.

Content Editing and Proofreading

Make sure your clients always get flawless work by using ChatGPT to help with editing and proofreading. Improve your clients' writing while raising your own output and earning potential by including AI-generated content suggestions alongside your human skills.

Search Engine Optimization

Use ChatGPT to produce search engine optimization (SEO)-friendly material for the benefit of individuals and organizations. You can earn money by giving an SEO-centric service to your clientele, in which you create content that enhances their organic traffic and profile online.

Speechwriting

Executives, politicians, and other public speakers can use ChatGPT to draft talks for their audiences. You may establish yourself as a competent speechwriter and land lucrative contracts by employing AI-generated content to create engaging and thought-provoking speeches.

Creative Writing

Use ChatGPT to generate short tales, poems, or even scripts and delve into the world of creative writing. There is a growing demand for distinctive and interesting literary content, and you may capitalize on this trend by providing creative writing services that are aided by artificial intelligence.

Content Licensing and Syndication

Produce professional-grade content with ChatGPT and sell licenses to companies and media outlets in need of new, interesting content. The need for unique and interesting material can be capitalized on in a passive manner by syndicating AI-generated content.

How to Monetize ChatGPT-Generated Content

As the use of AI in many industries continues to increase, ChatGPT has become a potent tool for content production, allowing business owners and content creators to make money in a variety of ways. Here, we'll look at ten different ways you can make money off of Your GPT content.

Affiliate Marketing

Promote the goods and services of other companies with the help of user-generated content from ChatGPT. Affiliate marketing is a terrific way to make money on the side while helping others by earning a commission on purchases made through your referral link.

Joint Ventures and Partnerships

Making connections with other creators or companies can lead to more ways to make money. You may turn your ChatGPT-generated content into marketable products and services by teaming together with others to produce things like collaborative e-books, courses, and workshops.

Earnings From Ads

Using advertising to monetize ChatGPT content might be a valuable business model. Your content can create a consistent stream of cash from the number of impressions or clicks on display adverts, sponsored content, or native advertising.

Digital Products

With ChatGPT, you can make and sell a variety of digital products, including e-books, webinars, and online courses. You can become known as an authority in your profession and make money from the sales of digital products if the content you provide is of high enough quality.

Premium Content and Courses

To develop premium material or courses with advanced learning chances, ChatGPT might be used. You can make more money from the people who are willing to pay for your knowledge and skills if you set the price of these products and services higher.

Services

One common strategy for making money from ChatGPT content is to offer related services, including customer assistance, writing, or content production. You can generate a continuous source of revenue by charging for your time and skills to solve problems on an individual or corporate level.

Templates and Resources

You can make money by using ChatGPT to make materials like resume samples, social media posts, and article outlines to sell to people who need help in these areas. You may monetize the content generated by your ChatGPT by providing high-quality, adaptable solutions to your users.

Audience Engagement

Speaking engagements and consultancy gigs are just two examples of how using content generated by ChatGPT might help you earn money. You may profit from the demand for your knowledge and create a devoted following by identifying yourself as an authority and doing the work necessary to do so.

Subscription-Based Services

A good method to make money off the content generated by ChatGPT is to provide a subscription-based service, like a newsletter or membership site. You can generate recurring income from your audience by charging a monthly or annual fee in exchange for regular updates, unique content, or membership to a helpful community.

Coaching and Mentorship

The insights and expertise gleaned from chat Chats can be used to provide coaching or mentoring. Helping customers overcome obstacles and reach their objectives will allow you to charge more for your services and generate more revenue.

Syndication and Licenses

You can also earn money from the content you create in ChatGPT by selling licenses or syndication rights to other services or media. To earn more money from your existing work, consider licensing it to third parties for republishing or distribution in exchange for royalties or fees.

Sponsored Posts and Collaborations

Working with companies to develop sponsored posts or collaborative material might be a successful method to monetize your ChatGPT activity. Sponsored content that adds value for your audience and benefits both you and your brand partners is possible through strategic relationships with businesses that fit your expertise and target demographic.

Chatbot Development

Businesses can utilize ChatGPT to create chatbots or virtual assistants to aid in customer service, sales, and information dissemination. You may make money off the creation, deployment, and maintenance of AI-powered chatbots by offering them as a service to corporations and other organizations.

Freelance Writing and Content Creation

Freelance writing and content production services can be offered to organizations and individuals using the ChatGPT-created material. You can charge more for your services and bring in money from a wide range of clients and projects if you provide high-quality, tailored content.

Merchandise and Physical Products

Making tangible things based on ChatGPT material is another way to make money off it. You could, for instance, make and sell t-shirts, posters, and other goods using phrases or images taken directly from your material. You can earn money and boost consumer confidence in your brand by selling these items to your target demographic.

Online Workshops and Training Sessions

Online workshops and training can benefit from the information generated by ChatGPT, which can be used to develop educational materials and tools. You can capitalize on your knowledge and the value of your content by charging a fee for workshops or sessions you deliver to your audience.

Patreon or Crowdfunding

Content developed by ChatGPT can also be sold on crowdfunding sites like Patreon. You may keep making great content for your audience and gain their continued financial support by offering them access to special content, benefits, or rewards in exchange for their contributions.

Content Marketplace

Another method to make money with your ChatGPT is to sell the material you produce on content marketplaces like Constant Content or ClearVoice. You can earn money from each piece of content you sell if you provide it to businesses or individuals who need content for their websites, blogs, or promotional materials.

Email Marketing

Newsletters, promotional emails, and autoresponders are just some of the types of email content that might benefit from using ChatGPT. You can earn money with email marketing by collecting email addresses from interested parties and regularly giving them content that is of value to them.

Data Analysis and Consulting

With ChatGPT, one may conduct data analysis, spot patterns, and come up with insights that can then be turned into consultancy or advising fees. You may earn money from your ChatGPT-created content by providing analysis and insights to businesses and organizations in exchange for a fee.

Chapter 9

ChatGPT Best Practices

Using the power of technologies like ChatGPT may dramatically improve communication, content creation, and research in this age of quickly developing AI technology. Of course, mastering the proper and effective use of such a potent resource is essential. To help readers use ChatGPT in a responsible and productive manner, we've included a chapter titled "ChatGPT Best Practices" We will explore the inner workings of this robust AI language model in order to help you maximize its potential and reduce its hazards.

In this chapter, we will discuss a variety of strategies, such as keeping up with the latest AI news and developments, which will help you keep pace with the rapidly developing field of AI. We'll also go over some basic security and privacy precautions you can take using ChatGPT to keep your data and the data of your users safe.

Getting the desired results from ChatGPT relies heavily on the skill of prompt engineers. I'll help you develop questions that provide you with answers that are precise, illuminating, and interesting.

Understanding where ChatGPT stops being useful is just as crucial, and I'll show you how to do it so you can avoid any unintended consequences.

The needs and difficulties of various sectors of the economy are different. The best results can be achieved through a discussion about how to optimize ChatGPT for various sectors, allowing you to shape the AI to meet your specific requirements. Finally, we'll cover some of the most typical pitfalls people encounter while using ChatGPT, so you can avoid those hiccups and get the most out of this robust linguistic framework.

At the end of this chapter, you will have a firm grasp of how to make the most efficient and ethical use of ChatGPT. These guidelines are intended to help anyone who uses ChatGPT do so ethically and successfully, whether they are content creators, researchers, or AI enthusiasts. Let's take this exciting step forward together and learn how to use ChatGPT to its full potential.

Staying Up to Date With AI News and Updates

Writers, content creators, and professionals utilizing AI technologies like ChatGPT must keep abreast of innovations in the field of AI, which is always expanding at a dizzying rate. Users can get the most out of AI-powered products in their workflows and remain ahead of the curve by keeping up with AI news and upgrades. Here, we'll go through why it's so crucial to stay abreast of AI developments and offer some suggestions for how to do just that.

Recognizing the Most Recent AI Advancements

New algorithms, tools, and application cases frequently emerge in the ever-changing AI world. By staying up to date on these developments, authors and content producers may better grasp how AI will affect their work and see opportunities to integrate cutting-edge AI technologies like ChatGPT into their workflows. Because of this, they can increase output, think outside the box, and create content that truly resonates with their audience.

Following Industry Publications

Following trade journals that report on developments in artificial intelligence is a great method to keep up with the field. Blogs authored by professionals in the area, authoritative publications dedicated to AI, and tech news websites are all good places to start. You may easily stay on top of developments in AI by subscribing to newsletters from the aforementioned resources.

Attending Conferences and Workshops

Conferences and workshops are great places to find out about the newest developments in AI, make connections with other experts in the industry, and network with other professionals. Attending these gatherings allows writers and content creators to expand their knowledge of AI, discover novel uses for ChatGPT and other technologies, and gain insight into how to incorporate AI most effectively into their work.

Participating in Virtual Communities and Forums

Taking part in AI-related online discussion groups and communities is a great way to keep up with the field and connect with people who share your interests. Members can talk about the latest findings, AI tools, and possible uses for these topics with other people in the community, all while learning from one another and expanding their horizons. Subreddits, LinkedIn groups, and specialist forums devoted to artificial intelligence have attracted large online communities.

Engaging With AI Researchers and Professionals on Social Media

In order to stay abreast of the newest developments in the field of artificial intelligence, it can be helpful to follow researchers, professionals, and companies working in this area on social media sites like Twitter and LinkedIn. Communicating with these groups and individuals can assist writers and content producers in learning more about AI and tools like ChatGPT.

Participating in Online Courses and Webinars

Users can improve their familiarity with AI technology and their potential uses by participating in online courses and webinars devoted to the subject. If you're interested in keeping up with AI developments, you can enroll in one of the many courses offered by universities, AI groups, and specialists in the subject.

Setting Up AI News Alerts

Setting up individualized news notifications is another useful strategy for keeping abreast of AI developments. You can stay on top of the newest AI advances with the help of tools like Google Alerts, which will send you relevant news and articles based on the keywords you specify.

Maintaining Security and Privacy

It is imperative that authors, content creators, and professionals emphasize security and privacy while working with ChatGPT and other AI-powered tools as their use becomes more widespread across industries. When dealing with private or proprietary information, it is crucial to take certain precautions. Here, we'll delve into why it's crucial to protect sensitive information while using ChatGPT and give you some practical advice on how to do just that.

Understanding the Significance of Security and Privacy Using ChatGPT

Despite ChatGPT's useful features, data security is crucial to maximizing the app's potential. Data breaches, illegal access to confidential information, and legal trouble could result from a failure to take these precautions. Users can lessen the likelihood of these accidents and maintain regulatory compliance in their ChatGPT operations by placing a premium on security and privacy.

Protecting Sensitive Information

Strong, unique passwords and, if users should use available, Multi-Factor Authentication (MFA) to secure their ChatGPT accounts and any other accounts or platforms connected to ChatGPT. Passwords that are more difficult to crack include a combination of upper and lowercase letters, numerals, and special characters. With multi-factor authentication, users are required to submit more than one form of identity before gaining access to a resource. This could be a fingerprint and a verification code delivered to a mobile device, for example.

Data Encryption

Information security relies heavily on the use of encryption, both during storage and transmission. Users can safeguard sensitive information by encrypting it so that only authorized parties have access to the decryption keys. Users should choose an encryption tool or protocol that is both suitable for their needs and compatible with ChatGPT from the several that exist.

Using Data Storage and Sharing Best Practices

In order to keep sensitive information safe and private while using ChatGPT, it is essential to follow best practices for data storage and exchange. Some examples are:

- Keeping files in a safe place, such as a cloud storage service with strong password protection and encryption features

- Backing up data on a regular basis to avoid loss or corruption

- Restricting access to data to only those who need it to do their jobs

- Safe information exchange via encrypted file-sharing services and other safe means

- Implementing regular software and system updates and patches to close security loopholes

Having a Firm Grasp of the Rules and Regulations in Effect

ChatGPT users should be aware of any laws or regulations that might affect their usage of AI technologies or their management of private information. The EU's General Data Protection Regulation (GDPR) is one example of a data protection policy that places stringent standards on the handling and storage of individual data. Users are responsible for understanding the laws in their region and acting in accordance with them when using ChatGPT.

Maintaining a Schedule of Routine Security Checks

Users should routinely review the security of ChatGPT to keep data secure and private. This could entail checking in on access controls, keeping an eye out for security holes, and making sure that everything is as secure as it can be. Protecting sensitive information and remaining in compliance with legal and regulatory mandates depends on users being aware of, and taking measures to mitigate, any security risks to which it may be exposed.

Training and Awareness

Finally, it is crucial that all team members who use ChatGPT receive enough training and are familiar with security and privacy best practices. Team members must be made aware of the legal and regulatory constraints that affect their use of AI technologies, the significance of using strong passwords, and the value of storing and sharing data securely.

Prompt Engineering

Prompt engineering is crucial in the field of artificial intelligence language models like ChatGPT since it allows us to fully exploit the capabilities of these tools to produce high-quality, novel results. Crafting high-quality prompts is the focus of prompt engineering, which allows users to train ChatGPT to respond as desired. This improves the bot's efficiency and makes it more flexible for use in a variety of settings. To help users learn this crucial skill and get the most out of ChatGPT, we'll dive into the fundamentals of prompt engineering here.

Understanding the Significance of Prompt Engineering

Prompt engineering, at its foundation, is all about getting the most out of ChatGPT by providing it with the finest possible input. When it comes to the usefulness and accuracy of the responses produced by AI language models like ChatGPT, the quality of the input is key. ChatGPT's overall efficacy can be improved by its users by tailoring the tool's prompts and methods to produce results that meet their needs and expectations.

Utilizing Specific Keywords and Phrases

Strategic usage of keywords and phrases is a cornerstone of prompt engineering. ChatGPT's responses can be heavily steered by the user by using pertinent terms and expressions in the prompt. This ensures that the generated material is relevant to the user and stays on-topic. The model needs some level of guidance, but it's also crucial not to stifle its imagination with unnecessary restrictions.

Asking Open-Ended Questions

Asking ChatGPT open-ended questions is another useful prompt engineering strategy. Users can train AI to produce more detailed and nuanced answers by providing it with more complex scenarios and context. When looking for specifics or a larger view of a topic, open-ended questions on ChatGPT allow for the exploration of multiple angles and the provision of nuanced insights.

Providing Context and Background Information

Providing appropriate context and background information in the prompt is critical for maximizing the relevance and accuracy of ChatGPT's output. Users can effectively lead the AI toward producing content that corresponds with their wants and expectations by providing a clear framework and describing any unique requirements. Provide information that can assist in framing your response, such as the intended audience, the tone or style you'd like to use, and so on.

Experimenting With Different Prompt Structures

Iteratively trying out different prompt structures until one produces the desired result is a common part of the prompt engineering process. Users may need to try out a few different options before settling on the best way to direct ChatGPT, such as rephrasing the prompt, increasing or decreasing the level of specificity, or switching up the question style. Users can optimize their input over time to get the best potential results from the AI by experimenting with different versions of the prompts.

Setting Output Length and Managing Verbosity

By adjusting a few settings, ChatGPT users can limit the amount of output they receive. Users can control how much detail is included in their responses by modifying this parameter. Depending on the situation and goal of the generated information, it is critical to find the right medium between succinctness and detail.

Evaluating and Refining the Output

Evaluating ChatGPT's output and making adjustments where appropriate is an essential component of the rapid engineering process. Adjusting the question or revising the generated content may be necessary to address any issues with clarity, coherence, or correctness. By constantly evaluating and refining the output, consumers can guarantee that the content is up to par with their expectations.

Understanding the Limitations of ChatGPT

It is vital to understand the limitations of ChatGPT, just as it is important to understand the limitations of any other technology, in order to utilize it effectively and avoid potential issues. The ChatGPT artificial intelligence language model is quite impressive, as it is able to generate text of high quality in a range of styles and tones. Yet, there are still limits to what it is capable of doing and how well it can function in a variety of settings and circumstances.

Accuracy is one of the most significant shortcomings of ChatGPT. Even though it is quite good at creating text, the results it produces are not guaranteed to be correct or dependable. This is especially true in circumstances in which the data that is being fed into it is unclear or insufficient. It is essential to be aware of this and to take measures to verify the accuracy of the output. This can be done by fact-checking the information or by collaborating with human editors who are able to provide additional context and information.

Another drawback of ChatGPT is its inherent bias. As is the case with all other language models, ChatGPT is trained on huge datasets. It is possible for these datasets to have inherent biases, and these biases may be represented in the output. This can be especially troublesome in scenarios in which the text created by ChatGPT may be used to make significant decisions or judgments, like in recruiting circumstances or legal contexts, where accurate information is essential. In order to alleviate the effects of this problem, it is essential to take the necessary precautions to ensure that the data being input is as varied and representative as is humanly possible and to carefully examine the results for any possible biases.

When utilizing ChatGPT, context is another key element to keep in mind. Although it is capable of producing high-quality content on a wide variety of subjects, it may have difficulty doing so in circumstances in which the context is unclear or convoluted. For instance, it might not be able to correctly discern nuances of tone or meaning, and it might also have trouble understanding cultural references and idioms. In order to solve this problem, it is essential to provide as much context as is reasonably possible when creating prompts or inputs, and it is also essential to carefully examine the output in order to guarantee that it is appropriate and accurate.

Last but not least, it is essential to be aware of the constraints that are imposed by ChatGPT when it comes to the generation of text in a variety of distinct styles and formats. It is possible that it will not be as effective in certain circumstances, such as poetry or extremely technical writing, despite the fact that it is able to generate text in a wide variety of styles and tones. In these kinds of circumstances, it may be required to make use of other AI tools or to collaborate with human editors in order to accomplish what has to be done.

Fine-Tuning ChatGPT for Specific Industries

It is a vital best practice to fine-tune ChatGPT for specific sectors, and doing so can assist content creators and authors in producing output that is more accurate and relevant to their intended audience. It is essential to keep in mind that there is not a single model that can be utilized for all situations, despite the fact that ChatGPT is a strong tool that can be put to a diverse set of purposes. Producing high-quality content requires being familiar with the lingo, terminologies, and subtleties of one's particular industry, many of which have their own vocabulary. As a result, adjusting ChatGPT for certain fields or applications like healthcare, banking, or e-commerce can be an efficient way to guarantee accurate and applicable results.

Doing fine-tuning on ChatGPT entails training the model on certain data sets and making use of tailored prompts or inputs in order to produce the required output. This can be accomplished by supplying the model with examples that are unique to the domain, as well as by developing prompts that are adapted to the particular field of endeavor or application. For instance, in the field of medicine, ChatGPT can be customized to deliver precise and up-to-date medical information to patients based on their symptoms, including possible diagnoses and treatment choices. In the field of finance, ChatGPT can be customized to provide many types of financial advice, such as recommendations for investments and plans for retirement planning. When it comes to online retail, ChatGPT has the capability of being fine-tuned to deliver individualized product recommendations to customers based on their browsing and purchasing history.

Customizing ChatGPT entails assembling a dataset reflective of the domain-specific expertise needed by a given field. This data set should go through a comprehensive curation process to ensure that it contains information that is both relevant and of high quality. When the data set has finished being processed, it will be ready for use in the machine-learning techniques needed to train the ChatGPT model. During this step of the process, the model's weights and parameters are modified so that it more accurately represents reality and is more applicable to the sector.

It is essential to keep in mind that the fine-tuning of ChatGPT calls for expert-level knowledge and experience in the fields of machine learning and natural language processing. As a result, it is possible that it will be necessary to work with a group of specialists or to employ a company that specializes in handling the process of fine-tuning the model.

Even though the process of fine-tuning ChatGPT might be time-consuming and difficult, it does offer a number of benefits to those who create material and compose it. To begin, it has the potential to assist in enhancing the precision and applicability of the product, making it more valuable for particular fields of endeavor or applications. Second, it may help cut down on the time and effort spent on manual editing and proofreading. Finally, it may assist in establishing the writer or content producer as an expert in a particular field, which may result in an increase in the number of business prospects as well as an increase in credibility.

Avoiding Mistakes When Using ChatGPT

In this part, we'll go over some of the most typical pitfalls that users encounter while utilizing ChatGPT, as well as potential solutions to these issues.

Over-Reliance on Results Without Adequate Scrutiny and Editing

Relying too heavily on the output without sufficient review or modification is one of the most typical mistakes made while using

ChatGPT. ChatGPT can produce high-quality content rapidly, but it must be reviewed and edited to guarantee accuracy, appropriateness, and audience demands. If you don't, you risk having inaccurate or misleading information spread about you, which can hurt your brand.

Set aside time for evaluation and editing after utilizing ChatGPT to prevent making this error. To verify that the output is accurate and acceptable may entail employing additional AI technologies or collaborating with human editors. To ensure that the information is of the greatest caliber, you should also be ready to make changes or updates as necessary.

Neglecting to Address Concerns About Bias or Accuracy

Failure to appropriately address questions of bias or accuracy is another typical blunder while using ChatGPT. Like any other artificial intelligence tool, ChatGPT is only as good as the data used to train it. The result produced by ChatGPT may potentially be biased or erroneous if the data is inaccurate.

To avoid this error, it is essential to carefully consider the data used to train ChatGPT and to address any bias or accuracy concerns. To train ChatGPT, employ varied data sets, multiple data sources, or consult experts.

Neglecting to Think About the Content's Ethical Consequences

The ethical implications of the material should also be taken into account when using ChatGPT. When used improperly or without due consideration of ethical issues, ChatGPT has the potential to produce content that is deceptive, offensive, or hurtful.

To prevent this blunder, users should give serious consideration to the ethical implications of the content produced by ChatGPT and take necessary precautions to prevent any harm. Experts in the field may be consulted; probable audience reactions weighed, and compliance with applicable laws and regulations taken into account.

Substituting for Human Judgment and Creativity

Last but not least, it's vital to remember that ChatGPT is not a substitute for human creativity and judgment. ChatGPT can rapidly and efficiently produce high-quality content, but it cannot replace human ingenuity and discretion. If you rely too heavily on ChatGPT, you risk producing bland, uninteresting content that lacks the originality and creativity necessary for effective communication.

To avoid this pitfall, utilize ChatGPT sparingly and as one of many tools in your content development arsenal. This might be using ChatGPT to spark ideas or inspiration but then using your own insight and imagination to flesh out the content. By doing so, you can guarantee that the content you create is of the greatest caliber and accurately captures your distinct voice and viewpoint.

Chapter 10

The Impact of ChatGPT and Its Future

As artificial intelligence continues to develop and evolve, the impact it has on various industries is becoming more apparent. One area that has seen significant growth and potential is AI language models, such as ChatGPT. In this chapter, we will examine the current state of ChatGPT and explore emerging trends in the development and application of AI language models. We will also provide predictions for how ChatGPT may evolve in the future and its potential impact on writing and communication.

To begin, we will discuss the positive impact of ChatGPT, including its ability to assist in content creation, research, and fact-checking. We will also explore its potential to improve accessibility and inclusivity in communication.

However, as with any technology, there are also negative aspects to consider. We will examine the potential ethical concerns and biases that may arise from the use of ChatGPT, as well as the potential impact on employment in the writing and content creation industries.

Next, we will explore potential advancements in ChatGPT technology, including the development of multilingual models and the integration of visual and audio elements. We will also discuss how ChatGPT can be fine-tuned for specific industries or use cases, such as healthcare or e-commerce.

Finally, we will examine the future of AI language models, including predictions for how ChatGPT and other AI tools may continue to evolve and be integrated into various industries. We will discuss the potential benefits and challenges that may arise from this continued development and how society can prepare for the future impact of AI language models.

The Positive Impact of ChatGPT

ChatGPT has the potential to revolutionize the way that we produce and consume content, making it faster and more efficient.

The capacity of ChatGPT to drastically speed up the content generation process is one of its main advantages. ChatGPT can help businesses and individuals create more content in less time by generating material at lightning speed, which can enhance productivity and output. Fast turnaround times are crucial in content-heavy industries like journalism and media. Thus, this might be very helpful. Writers and bloggers, for example, can use ChatGPT to increase output and meet deadlines. Ultimately, ChatGPT can aid in making content production easier and more accessible for everyone.

Improve accessibility and help to break down barriers to information.

ChatGPT's potential to remove information access obstacles and increase accessibility is another significant advantage. The flexibility of ChatGPT means that it can be used to generate material in a wide range of languages and file formats, making it more accessible to people from many walks of life. Those who aren't native speakers of a language or who have limitations may benefit greatly from this. In addition, ChatGPT can make difficult content easier to read and comprehend, making it available to a larger audience.

Improve the quality of content

By creating information that is both accurate and pertinent to the user's demands, ChatGPT can aid in the enhancement of content quality. This is especially helpful in fields like healthcare and finance, where accuracy and precision are crucial. By using ChatGPT, you can make sure that everyone is using the most recent data and research. In order to ensure that the data supplied is as accurate as possible, ChatGPT can also help to lower the possibility of human error.

The potential to make text-based interfaces more accessible

ChatGPT can be a useful tool for persons with impairments since it makes it easier for them to communicate and obtain information through text-based interfaces. Those who have trouble communicating due to vision or hearing issues may benefit greatly from this. ChatGPT can help level the playing field so that people from all walks of life have equal opportunities to learn and grow.

Automate customer care and assistance

ChatGPT can be used to automate customer care and assistance, which can speed up response times and shorten client wait times. For companies that receive a lot of calls or run around the clock, this can be extremely helpful. As a result of receiving prompt and precise responses to their questions, customers are less likely to become frustrated, and their level of satisfaction is higher.

Create more inclusive and diverse content

By generating material in multiple languages and from a variety of views, ChatGPT can aid in the development of more inclusive and diverse content. For companies or groups trying to reach a larger audience, this can be extremely helpful. Conversational GPT can assist in ensuring that content is given in a way that is understandable and interesting to a wide range of users, independent of their background or cultural setting. Moreover, ChatGPT can assist in ensuring that a variety of viewpoints are reflected in the content, making it more engaging and educational for all readers.

ChatGPT can help with language acquisition and translation in addition to the benefits already discussed. ChatGPT can help people learn new languages or translate content from one language to another by generating text in several languages. This has the potential to reduce language barriers and enhance cross-cultural communication.

By producing reports and summaries based on enormous volumes of data, ChatGPT can also help scientists examine and draw conclusions more quickly. In sectors like medicine, environmental science, and social sciences, this may have a big influence.

The Negative Aspects of ChatGPT

May perpetuate biases

One of the main issues with ChatGPT is that it has the ability to reinforce existing biases in the data it uses to learn, which could have detrimental repercussions for historically oppressed groups. This is due to the fact that ChatGPT can only produce accurate results if it is fed high-quality, undistorted input.

For instance, if the data used to train ChatGPT is biased against a certain race or gender, the output produced by ChatGPT may likewise reflect similar biases. In areas like healthcare and the judicial system, where biased algorithms could lead to discriminatory actions, this has potentially devastating consequences.

To solve this issue, researchers and developers are looking into ways to reduce bias in AI algorithms, such as diversifying the data sets used to train them or creating algorithms that can identify and adjust for bias in real-time.

Generating fake news or propaganda

The use of ChatGPT to spread false information or propaganda is another potential drawback. ChatGPT's ability to generate convincing and coherent prose opens the door for its usage in the creation of convincing false news stories or propaganda pieces that can be extensively spread online.

This is especially worrisome in today's society, where misinformation is rampant, and faith in institutions is dwindling. The use of ChatGPT to spread false information or propaganda can exacerbate these issues, further eroding trust and endangering the legitimacy of crucial organizations like the media or the government.

To counteract this problem, it's crucial to provide tools and strategies that can identify and highlight bogus news generated by ChatGPT. It's also crucial to teach the public about the dangers of AI-generated fake news and the necessity of double-checking the veracity of any material before accepting it as fact.

The potential to replace human workers

Furthermore, another potential drawback of ChatGPT is that it may eventually replace human labor in some industries, which would result in job loss and economic inequity. This is especially worrisome in sectors where ChatGPT has the potential to automate many functions that were previously performed by people, like customer service or content development.

While automation has the potential to boost productivity and efficiency, it can also have negative effects on workers who might lose their jobs. The economic disparity may result from this, as individuals who are able to adopt new technologies and find jobs in emerging industries may fare better than those who are left behind.

To solve this problem, we need to design policies and programs that assist employees in making the transition to new industries and acquiring the knowledge and abilities necessary to thrive in the 21st-century economy. Policies like universal basic income or job retraining programs can help ensure that the benefits of automation are distributed more equitably.

The inherent privacy implications of ChatGPT are still another potential drawback. There is a chance that private or sensitive information could be accidentally disclosed or misused as technology advances. If ChatGPT is used for customer support, for instance, there is a possibility that sensitive client data will be leaked or exploited.

The use of ChatGPT also begs the question of who owns and controls the created content. Who is liable for any mistakes or inaccuracies in the output, and who owns the intellectual property rights to the created content? When ChatGPT is used to produce content for commercial or legal purposes, these problems can become especially intricate.

Concerns have also been raised that the widespread use of ChatGPT could lead to a decline in human creativity and inventiveness. There is a danger that the human perspective and creativity that underpin many types of communication will be lost as more and more content is generated by AI language models.

The ethical ramifications of ChatGPT use are also not widely understood. Concerns have been raised concerning the possibility of ChatGPT being used for illegal purposes, including creating fictitious identities for online fraud or cyberattacks. The employment of ChatGPT in military or government settings also presents serious ethical concerns about the possibility of power abuse and misuse.

Finally, there is the worry that ChatGPT could develop too much, ushering in a dark future when machines outsmart people and take over civilization. This is a common theme in science fiction, and while it may sound fantastical, it is vital to think about the consequences of the continuous development of artificial intelligence language models like ChatGPT.

Notwithstanding these drawbacks, it's worth remembering that many of them can be avoided through regulation and ethical considerations. Stakeholders in ChatGPT development and deployment should weigh the technology's benefits against its hazards and take precautions to reduce any unfavorable effects. By doing so, we can ensure that ChatGPT continues to have a beneficial impact on how we communicate and access information while avoiding any potential drawbacks.

Potential Advancements in ChatGPT Technology

The accuracy, speed, and efficiency could potentially improve

Like with any technology, ChatGPT is expected to witness advancements in its core algorithms and functionality over time. This could result in speedier response times and improved content generation accuracy. Hardware advancements, such as faster processors or more memory, may also contribute to improving ChatGPT's speed and efficiency.

Potentially evolve to be more flexible

ChatGPT is currently trained on a big dataset of general language patterns, making it a flexible tool that may be applied to a variety of contexts. But, as the technology evolves, it may become more configurable, allowing users to tailor the model to specific sectors like healthcare or banking. This has the potential to produce output that is more precise and pertinent to the requirements of those businesses.

Achieve a more streamlined and effective content creation process

As AI technology develops, ChatGPT is anticipated to become more integrated with other AI tools and technologies. To better grasp context or identify sentiment, for instance, it might be combined with NLP techniques. ChatGPT could generate first drafts that are subsequently edited by other tools and/or human editors, leading to a more streamlined and efficient content creation process.

Increasingly hard to distinguish AI-generated content form human-generated content

It's possible that as ChatGPT technology develops, the output it produces will become more natural and human-like. This could make it more challenging to tell AI-generated content from human-produced content. This may have many positive outcomes, but it may also have unfavorable ones, such as promoting false information or devaluing people's time and effort.

May evolve to produce more varied content, including images and movies, in addition to text.

Today, ChatGPT is largely used to create text-based content. Nevertheless, as technology develops, it's possible that it may be used to produce other kinds of information, like pictures or films. This may open up new avenues for artistic expression and content production, but it may also pose new ethical questions, such as the possibility of the abuse of AI-generated images or movies.

Also, as ChatGPT develops, it may become more malleable and applicable to a wider variety of contexts. In order to increase the model's ability to produce accurate and pertinent information for a specific field, this may entail putting domain-specific knowledge into the model. To deliver more precise diagnoses and treatment recommendations, a Specialized GPT model created specifically for healthcare may be trained on medical jargon and patient data.

Integration of other AI tools and technologies is another potential development in ChatGPT technology. Natural language processing could be used to improve ChatGPT's comprehension of spoken language. To enhance the model's capacity for learning and adaptation over time, it may also require using machine learning techniques.

There may be a transition toward more natural and human-like communication as ChatGPT technology develops. This may entail providing the model with additional context so that it can recognize and appropriately respond to a wider range of human emotions and linguistic complexity. This would make ChatGPT's output more consistent and difficult to tell from human-generated stuff.

Last but not least, ChatGPT has the ability to provide material other than text. A ChatGPT model trained to generate photos, for instance, may produce one-of-a-kind visuals in response to user input, while a ChatGPT model trained to generate videos could provide personalized motion pictures. This might provide writers, marketers, and other professionals with a wealth of fresh inspiration.

Future of AI-Language Models

The future of AI language models is anticipated to feature additional breakthroughs in correctness, relevance, and natural language processing. More precision, fewer mistakes, and higher output quality are all possible with the ongoing development of AI language models. Conversations with future models are anticipated to be more natural and human-like since they will be better able to understand the context of the dialogue. As time goes on, advances in natural language processing will allow artificial intelligence language models to comprehend and react to increasingly nuanced linguistic structures and patterns.

A more streamlined and effective user experience could be achieved by integrating AI language models with other technologies like virtual assistants and chatbots. AI language models will become more intertwined with other technologies as they progress. A more smooth and more natural user experience, as well as improved task and information management, will be made possible by this connection.

AI language models may also improve their capacity to recognize and express emotions, which could result in more compelling and tailored content. As AI language models advance, they might be better able to recognize and react to linguistic expressions of emotion. This has the potential to lead to more interesting and relevant material that is specifically suited to the demands and emotional states of each user.

The ability to analyze and explain the model's output may become more important in the future of artificial intelligence language models. Transparency and interpretability will become more and more important as AI language models spread. Because of this, customers will have a better understanding of the model's decision-making process, which should inspire more faith in the innovation.

As AI language models become more sophisticated, regulatory scrutiny and oversight may increase to guarantee that they are used responsibly and ethically. There will be a need for regulation and governance to ensure that AI language models are used in an ethical and responsible manner, given their potential to have significant societal effects.

ChatGPT and other AI technologies may one day aid in achieving Singularity as AI language models advance at a rate never before seen. Singularity is a hypothetical time in the distant future when artificial intelligence develops to the point where it can compete with human intelligence. Although this idea is still in its infancy and fraught with uncertainty, the fast-paced advancement of AI language models and other AI technologies is prompting serious reflection on the place of artificial intelligence in society.

AI language models are anticipated to become more widely available to a variety of people and organizations as they continue to progress. This has the potential to contribute to a democratization of content development by leveling the playing field between giant media conglomerates and smaller firms.

The risk of misusing or abusing AI language models, however, increases with their democratization. There may be times when people or organizations utilize these tools for bad, such as propagating lies or propaganda. In order to ensure that AI language models are utilized ethically and responsibly, it will be crucial for regulatory organizations to set norms and legislation pertaining to their use.

More public awareness and education about the potential and

limitations of AI language models may be necessary in addition to regulatory supervision. This can aid in debunking misconceptions and encouraging the responsible and informed application of these technologies.

In general, the prospects for AI language models like ChatGPT are both promising and murky. There are important ethical and societal challenges that need to be addressed, even though these technologies have the potential to revolutionize the way in which information is produced and consumed. We can make sure that the influence of AI language models is beneficial and useful for everyone by recognizing these issues and working together to find solutions.

Ethical Considerations

As AI language models continue to progress, there are an increasing number of ethical considerations that need to be taken into account. Some of these considerations include bias and privacy problems. AI language models are only as good as the data they are trained on, and if the data contains biases, those biases will be mirrored in the output of the model. For instance, if a ChatGPT model is trained on data that is predominantly authored by white men, it may struggle to generate correct and relevant output for users who belong to other demographic groups. This can have repercussions in the actual world, such as reinforcing prejudices and disparities.

It is essential for the people who develop ChatGPT, as well as those who use it, to be aware of these ethical problems and to take action to lessen the damage that they have. This could entail employing various training data sets that are representative of different demographic groups, guaranteeing transparency in the content development process, and being aware of any privacy infringement. For instance, developers can take precautions like anonymizing user data and gaining the users' express approval before utilizing it to train language models.

The ethical questions raised by ChatGPT are not limited to the content that it produces; rather, they encompass a wider range of topics, such as the consumption of energy and the emissions of carbon dioxide that are involved with the training and operation of big language models. The enormous amount of computing power that is required to train and run large language models like ChatGPT can have a substantial impact on the environment. It is crucial for users and developers of ChatGPT to be aware of this impact and to investigate ways to reduce energy usage, such as adopting renewable energy sources or optimizing code in order to reduce the amount of computational work that is required.

In addition, it is essential for users of ChatGPT to be aware of the potential unintended implications, which may include the perpetuation of harmful stereotypes or the reinforcement of biases that already exist. For instance, ChatGPT may provide results that are offensive or discriminating, even if the user did not intend for them to do so. It is essential for users to carefully analyze and revise the output that is generated by ChatGPT in order to ensure that it is accurate, pertinent, and free from damaging prejudices or stereotypes.

When working with ChatGPT, privacy problems are also a key ethical consideration that must be taken into consideration. In order to train and produce reliable output, language models like ChatGPT need access to vast volumes of user data. However, this data might include private information like names, addresses, financials, or health records. It is essential for the developers of ChatGPT and users of the platform to be aware of these privacy problems and to take measures to protect user data, such as encrypting user data and imposing stringent data access rules.

Competitors of ChatGPT

Even while ChatGPT has gained a lot of attention, the fact that it is so widely used has rendered it unreliable for day-to-day use because it frequently reaches its maximum capacity. The good news is that there are a large number of AI chatbots that are available whenever you require them and have the same level of capability as you do.

ChatSonic API

ChatSonic API is a new pre-trained dialogue creation algorithm for multi-turn chats combined with Google for better outcomes on any topic. Writesonic's sophisticated chatbot responds quickly to your requests for material by providing up-to-date information, voice searches, and photos. ChatSonic provides access to a vast body of information as well as chats, and it never forgets anything a user has spoken.

The powerful artificial intelligence chatbot developed by Writesonic can generate content requirements by leveraging input from blogs, long-form articles, or Facebook advertising material. The tool has been taught to provide responses in the form of conversations, making it a great tool for use in customer support operations. It is possible to integrate ChatSonic with Google in order to produce material that is incredibly relevant, truthful, and up to date on any subject that may be specified. The persona mode, for example, allows users to assume one of at least 16 different characters during a conversation.

Google Bard

In addition to ChatGPT, a newer alternative called Bard is on the rise; it is backed by Google's Linguistic Model for Dialog Applications (LaMDA) and comes with over 137 billion parameters and 1.56 trillion words in its training set. LaMDA is equipped with the most advanced Natural Language Processing features and has been meticulously adjusted based on three metrics: quality, safety, and groundedness.

The artificial intelligence-powered tool is intended to take input in natural language and provide responses that are content-aware as well as natural and cohesive. In addition, it offers a one-of-a-kind response to follow-up queries, which positions it as a viable alternative to ChatGPT.

At the moment, Bard is in the process of going through its pace in Google's artificial intelligence test kitchen. When their chatbot provided false information in a promotional ad in February, Alphabet shares fell. Is Google releasing a competition to ChatGPT a little bit too quickly?

Microsoft Bing AI

OpenAI, the company that developed ChatGPT, has benefited from Microsoft's financial backing for several years. As Microsoft witnessed the tremendous success that ChatGPT was having, the company decided to increase its investment in OpenAI to the tune of $10 billion.

In more recent times, Microsoft has made use of this cooperation in order to launch their very own generative AI product, which is known as Bing AI. Bing AI is intended to bring about increased accuracy, efficiency, and speed. The application was developed on top of a language model platform from OpenAI, which is said to be superior to both ChatGPT and GPT-3.

Microsoft Bing AI takes the most important learnings and improvements from the original Bing and applies them to produce even better search results. The company intends to incorporate chat and compose, two artificial intelligence features, into the Edge browser. The artificial intelligence tool developed by Microsoft is also receiving a great deal of bad news due to some very concerning replies. Although it does not appear that Bing AI is nearly ready for usage by the general public just yet, a limited version is now available for free while a more comprehensive version is awaiting.

Chinchilla

Chinchilla is a project developed by Deepmind and is regarded as the successor of GPT-3. It has various features and advantages in comparison to ChatGPT. Using the math MMLU data set, it was found to perform better than ChatGPT, despite having 70 billion parameters and being built on a transformer model similar to GPT-3 and BERT. So, Chinchilla is suitable for people who are interested in constructing more complex AI artwork, writing assignments, and search engines.

Chinchilla is still a relatively new product, despite the fact that it is three times larger than GPT-3, and interested consumers are required to contact Deepmind in order to gain access to it.

Amazon CodeWhisperer

The purpose of Amazon's Codewhisperer is to provide developers with an alternative method of discovering, comprehending, and debugging code bugs. The tool performs a study of the code, identifies trends and flaws, and provides an in-depth analysis of the action being performed by the code by utilizing natural language processing and sophisticated machine learning methods. The time and effort needed to respond to concerns can be decreased by using Codewhisperer, which can combine possible bugs and performance issues with advice for fixes.

For developers, Amazon Codewhisperer is an exceptionally intriguing piece of software, and this is especially true when one considers the numerous applications that developers have discovered for ChatGPT. It also connects with other programming tools, such as GitHub. The Amazon CodeWhisperer service is currently undergoing evaluation and is offered to developers at no cost (*5 ChatGPT competitors emerging in 2023*, 2023).

Jasper

In order to generate responses that are human-like, Jasper uses natural language processing just like ChatGPT does. Even more impressive is the fact that Jasper utilizes the same language model as ChatGPT, namely OpenAI's GPT-3, which was developed by the AI research company that was responsible for ChatGPT.

Like ChatGPT, Jasper can be instructed to write whatever you want it to by entering a prompt. The most notable distinction with Jasper is that it comes equipped with a wide variety of tools to help you write better text. Jasper can write in over fifty different templates, including blog articles, video scripts, Twitter threads, and more, and can check for grammar and plagiarism.

If you run a business that requires you to produce written content on a daily basis, Jasper is the tool you need. It is an investment, though, at $24 each month.

YouChat

Like ChatGPT and Jasper, YouChat employs GPT-3 from OpenAI. Like the free version of ChatGPT, Jasper allows you to input a prompt for the text you need written and then writes the text for you. Whatever you type into the chatbot will be answered, including translating, math, coding, and writing tasks. Because of its low popularity, this chatbot is always available to answer your questions.

Also, unlike ChatGPT, which lacks an internet connection, this chatbot provides links to relevant Google results. If you ask YouChat, "What is soda?" it will respond with a conversational text and quote sources from Google to explain where it got its information. The chatbot is exactly as useful, has no bothersome capacity limits, and is free (Ortiz, 2023).

Bloom

Hugging Face explains that BLOOM is an autoregressive Large Language Model (LLM) designed to continue text from a prompt on large volumes of text data utilizing industrial-scale computational resources. This means it can produce text in 46 languages and 13 computer languages that are logical and indistinguishable from human-written material. By recasting them as text generation tasks, BLOOM can be directed to carry out text activities it hasn't been specifically trained for.

There will be others who share your inability to differentiate between BLOOM and GPT. This did not happen by chance. To break Big Tech's monopoly on big data, BLOOM was born (Devanesh, 2022).

Conclusion

It is beyond a shadow of a doubt that as the field of artificial intelligence continues to make strides forward, AI language models like ChatGPT will play a more prominent part in the writing and content creation processes. As I conclude "The Revolutionary ChatGPT Guide," I hope you have received significant ideas and techniques for using ChatGPT and other AI language models in your work. We have explored the possible benefits of ChatGPT, such as improving the accessibility, quality, and inclusion of material, while also highlighting the problems and ethical considerations that come along with the use of this technology.

The possibility that ChatGPT will change the ways in which we produce and consume content is one of the most significant advantages it offers. ChatGPT is able to help speed up the process of creating material while simultaneously guaranteeing that the content is of a high-quality thanks to its capacity to provide information that is both accurate and relevant and that is tailored specifically to the needs of the user. In addition, ChatGPT can assist in promoting accessibility by offering content in a variety of languages and forms, hence removing obstacles to accessing information.

Yet, it is essential to keep in mind that the utilization of ChatGPT is accompanied by its own specific set of difficulties as well as ethical issues to consider. As we have covered in this book, ChatGPT may be responsible for perpetuating biases in the data that it is trained on, which can have a negative impact on communities that are marginalized. The use of ChatGPT for the purpose of manufacturing fake news or propaganda can likewise have serious and far-reaching implications, contributing to the spread of disinformation and weakening trust in institutions. Last but not least, the possibility that ChatGPT will replace human labor in certain industries may result in the loss of jobs and increased economic inequality.

It is essential to make responsible use of ChatGPT, which includes being aware of its restrictions and the various problems it may present. You can guarantee that you are getting the most out of this technology by following best practices, including fine-tuning the model, using high-quality prompts, and resolving concerns of bias and accuracy. By doing so, you can maximize the benefits of this technology. In addition, it is vital to keep in mind the potential outcomes and unforeseen effects that may result from the use of this technology. As users and creators, we have a continuing obligation to place a high priority on ethical issues and work toward the responsible development and application of AI language models.

When one takes a look into the future, there is no question that AI language models will continue to play a role that is increasingly crucial in the process of writing and the creation of content. We can anticipate much more substantial gains in technology as developments take place in areas such as precision, speed, and the processing of natural languages. Yet, as the usage of AI language models grows more pervasive, it is essential to maintain an awareness of the potential repercussions and unintended effects that may arise. As users and creators, we have a continuing obligation to place a high priority on ethical issues and work toward the responsible development and application of AI language models.

As you continue to investigate the opportunities presented by ChatGPT and other AI language models, I strongly suggest that you consult this book as both a guide and a reference. This technology has the potential to revolutionize the way in which you operate and interact with others, regardless of whether you work in content creation, marketing, or writing. You can use the power of ChatGPT to elevate your writing and content creation to new heights by keeping up with the most recent advances, learning from the experiences of others, and adhering to best practices.

Finally, I would like to offer my heartfelt appreciation to you for taking the time to read this book. I really hope that this book has helped you get some useful insights and tactics that will allow you to get the most out of ChatGPT and any other AI language models that you may be working with. If you think other people might benefit from reading about your experiences with this book, please consider writing a review and sharing it with them. I am looking forward to seeing the incredible things that you will produce in the future with ChatGPT and other cutting-edge technologies, and I wish you the best of luck as you go on your road to making a living with AI.

References

5 ChatGPT competitors emerging in 2023. (2023, March 9). Gigster. https://gigster.com/blog/5-chatgpt-competitors-emerging-in-2023/

Devanesh. (2022, December 31). *5 free ChatGPT competitors you should know about for 2023*. Geek Culture. https://medium.com/geekculture/5-free-chatgpt-competitors-you-should-know-about-for-2023-ff5fc48d0430

Noy, S., & Zhang, W. (2023). *Experimental evidence on the productivity effects of generative artificial intelligence*. MIT. https://economics.mit.edu/sites/default/files/inline-files/Noy_Zhang_1.pdf

Ortiz, S. (2023, April 12). *The best AI chatbots of 2023: ChatGPT and alternatives*. ZDNET. https://www.zdnet.com/article/best-ai-chatbot/

Made in the USA
Las Vegas, NV
06 October 2023